ESL Pathways

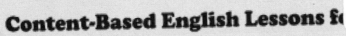

Content-Based English Lessons fo

Foundations
Beginner

Foundations is a beginner-level language-learning textbook for adult learners.

Features of this book include:

- 24 content-based conversation topics
- A wide variety of interesting subject matter
- Emphasis on comprehension and discussion
- Ideal for both individual and group instruction

Daniel Harrington   **Kimberly Heeren**   **David Treanor**

Foundations 1

English for Beginning Level Language Learners

By:

Daniel Harrington
Kimberly Heeren
David Treanor

Foundations
Beginner

Foundations is a beginner-level language-learning textbook for adult learners.

Features of this book include:

* 24 content-based conversation topics

* A wide variety of interesting subject matter

* Emphasis on comprehension and discussion

* Ideal for both individual and group instruction

Table of Contents

Characters in the Book:

- Kathy is a secretary in a law firm.

- Charles is a bank manager.

- Freddy is a high school teacher.

- Maria is a student.

- Patrick owns a restaurant.

- Anita is a housewife.

- John is a student.

- Marcia is a sales representative.

Meeting People

Look at these pictures. Say something about them.

Read about Kathy and Charles.

- Hi, my name is Kathy. I am a secretary. I work in an office. I have worked there for 5 years. I like my job very much. I like my boss and my co-workers.

  I am 27 years old. I have long blonde hair and blue eyes. I am 155 centimeters tall and I weigh 50 kilograms.

  I live in an apartment on Park Road. My phone number is 234-5678. I am single. I don't have a boyfriend. In my free time I like to go swimming. I also enjoy reading novels.

- Hello, my name is Charles. I am a bank manager. I work in an office, too. I have worked there for 20 years. I like my job very much, too. I like my boss and my co-workers.

  I am 54 years old. I have short, brown hair and brown eyes. I am 175 centimeters tall and I weigh 80 kilograms.

  I live in a house on Maple Street. My phone number is 695-3452. I am married. My wife's name is Susan. We have 2 children. We have one son and a daughter. When I have free time I like to play golf. I also like to play cards.

Dialogue: Kathy and Charles are talking.

Kathy: *Hi Charles, how are you?*
Charles: *Fine thanks, Kathy. How are you?*
Kathy: *I'm good. Do you still work at the bank?*
Charles: *Yes, I enjoy working there. And you? Do you still work in an office?*
Kathy: *Yes. I have been there for five years now. How are your children?*
Charles: *They are both fine, too.*
Kathy: *Well, I have to go home now. It was nice to see you, Charles.*
Charles: *Nice to see you, too, Kathy. Have a good day.*

Questions about Kathy:

1.   What is her name?
2.   What is her job?
3.   Where does she work?
4.   How long has she worked there?
5.   Does she like her job?
6.   How old is she?
7.   What does she look like?
8.   How tall is she?
9.   How much does she weigh?
10.   Where does she live?
11.   What's her phone number?
12.   Is Kathy married?
13.   Does she have a boyfriend?
14.   What does she like to do in her free time?

Questions about Charles:

1.   What's his name?
2.   What's his job?
3.   How long has he worked there?
4.   How old is he?
5.   What does he look like?
6.   How tall is he?
7.   How much does he weigh?
8.   Where does he live?
9.   What's his phone number?
10.   Is Charles married?
11.   Does he have any children?
12.   How many sons does he have?
13.   How many daughters does he have?
14.   What does he like to do when he has free time?

Activity: Personal Information

Fill in the blanks with information about yourself:

- My name is _____

- I am a _____

- I _____ at _____

- I am _____ years old

- I have _____ hair and _____ eyes

- I am _____ centimeters tall and I weigh _____ kilograms

- I live in a _____ on _____ in

  _____

- My phone number is _____

- I _____ married. I live with _____

- In my free time I like to _____ or _____

Discussion Questions: Ask your classmates these questions.

1.   What's your name?
2.   What do you do?
3.   Do you like it?
4.   How old are you?
5.   Describe your hairstyle.
6.   How tall are you?
7.   How much do you weigh?
8.   Where do you live?
9.   What's your phone number?

10.   Are you married?
11.   What do you like to do in your free time?
12.   Do you have a job? What do you do?
13.   How long have you had this job?
14.   What kinds of jobs are interesting to you?
15.   What kinds of jobs are not interesting to you?

Video Mania

Grammar Focus: Fill in the blanks.

Hi, my name _____ Kathy. I _____ a secretary. I _____ for a law firm. I

_____ in an office. I _____ there for 5 years. I _____ my job

very much. I _____ my boss and my co-workers.

I _____ 27 years old. I _____ short, blonde hair and blue eyes. I

_____ 155 centimeters tall and I _____ 50 kilograms.

I _____ in an apartment on Park Road. My _____ is 234-5678.

I _____ single. I _____ a boyfriend. In my free time I _____ to

go _____. I also enjoy _____ novels.

Lesson 2 — Families

Look at these pictures. Say something about each.

Anita and Patrick are talking about their families.

Anita: There are five people in my family. They are my husband, my eldest daughter, my youngest daughter, my son and me. My parents have four children. They have two sons and two daughters. I have three siblings. I have one older brother, one younger brother and one younger sister.

Patrick: There are four people in my family. They are my wife, my daughter, my son and me. My parents have three children. They have two daughters and one son. I have two siblings. I have one older sister and one younger sister.

Dialogue: Read the conversation between Anita and Patrick.

Anita: *Hi Patrick, how are you today?*
Patrick: *I'm fine thanks Anita, how are you?*
Anita: *Pretty good, thanks. How are your wife and children doing?*
Patrick: *They are fine. My wife is busy at work and my kids are busy at school.*
Anita: *How old are your children now?*
Patrick: *Well, our daughter is ten and our son is seven.*
Anita: *How are they doing at school?*
Patrick: *They both like school very much. How are your children doing?*
Anita: *They are all fine. Our eldest daughter is in junior high school now.*
Patrick: *How about your youngest daughter and your son?*
Anita: *Well, our youngest daughter is in elementary school and our son is in
         kindergarten.*
Patrick: *Do they like school?*
Anita: *Yes they do. They all enjoy going to school.*

Questions about Anita's family:

1. How many people are in Anita's family?
2. Who are they?
3. How many children does she have?
4. How many daughters does she have?
5. How many sons does she have?
6. How many children do her parents have?
7. How many sons do they have?
8. How many daughters do they have?
9. How many siblings does Anita have?
10. How many brothers does she have?
11. How many sisters does she have?

Questions about Patrick's family:

1. How many people are in Patrick's family?
2. Who are they?
3. How many children does he have?
4. How many daughters does he have?
5. How many sons does he have?
6. How many children do his parents have?
7. How many sons do they have?
8. How many daughters do they have?
9. How many siblings does Patrick have?
10. How many brothers does he have?
11. How many sisters does he have?

Activity: Family Trees

Look at the family trees of Anita and Patrick.

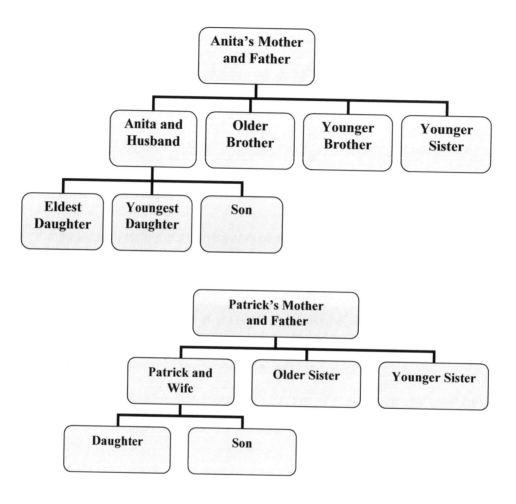

Use a large piece of paper. Draw a family tree for your family. Now draw one for your classmate's family. Show them to other students.

Discussion Questions:

1. How many people are in your family?
2. Who are they?
3. How many children do your parents have?
4. How many sons do they have?
5. How many daughters do they have?
6. How many siblings do you have?
7. How many brothers do you have?
8. How many sisters do you have?

9. Do you have any children?
10. How many children do you have?
11. How many daughters do you have?
12. How many sons do you have?
13. What do you and your family like to do together?
14. Where do you and your family like to go?
15. Who is the oldest person in your family?
16. Who is the youngest person in your family?

Grammar Focus: Fill in the blanks.

Anita : There are _____ people in my family. They are my _____, my elder

_____, my younger _____, my _____ and me. My parents have four

_____. They have two _____ and two _____. I have three

_____. I have one older _____, one younger _____ and

one younger _____.

Patrick : There are four _____ in my _____. They are my

_____, my _____, my _____ and me. My _____ have

three _____. They have two _____ and _____ son. I have

two _____. I have one _____ sister and one _____ sister.

Lesson 3	Jobs

Look at these pictures. Say something about each.

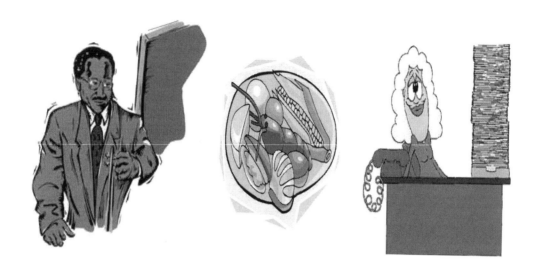

Read about some different people's jobs.

Freddy is a high school teacher. He teaches math and P.E. (physical education) at Carver High School. He likes his job very much. He has worked there for ten years. In math class Freddy teaches algebra to his students. In PE class Freddy and his students play different kinds of sports. He likes working with high school students but sometimes the job is tiring and he feels tired.

Patrick is a seafood restaurant owner. He has worked there for fifteen years. The restaurant was his father's before. His father retired and gave the restaurant to Patrick. He likes his job very much. His restaurant sells many different kinds of seafood. It sells fish, shrimp, oysters and other kinds of seafood. Patrick likes to be in the restaurant and serve fresh seafood to his customers, although, sometimes the seafood is a little smelly.

Marcia is a sales representative. She works in an office. She has worked there for seven years. She sells watches to department stores and to boutiques. She talks on the telephone and meets with her customers. She likes her job very much, however sometimes her throat is sore because she has to talk a lot.

Questions:

1. What is Freddy's job?
2. Where does he work?
3. What does he do at his job?
4. How long has he worked there?
5. Does he like his job?
6. What doesn't he like about his job?

7. What is Patrick's job?
8. Where does he work?
9. What does he do at his job?
10. How long has he worked there?
11. Does he like his job?
12. What doesn't he like about his job?

13. What is Marcia's job?
14. Where does she work?
15. What does she do at her job?
16. How long has she worked there?
17. Does she like her job?
18. What doesn't she like about her job?

Interview one of the people about their jobs. Work with a classmate. One student asks six questions. The other student should answer them.

Ask:	Classmate answers:
1. What is your job?	*I am a* _____.
2. Where do you work?	*I work at* _____.
3. What do you do at your job?	*I* _____ *and* _____.
4. How long have you worked there?	*I have worked there for* _____ *years.*
5. Do you like your job?	*I like my job* _____.
6. What don't you like about your job?	*Sometimes* _____.

Activity: Other People's Jobs

Think of some people you know. Write down some things about their jobs.

Name		
Where do they work?		
What is their job?		
What do they do?		
How long have they worked there?		
Do they like the job?		
What don't they like about it?		

Make a list of some indoor jobs and outdoor jobs.

Indoor jobs	Outdoor jobs

Discussion Questions:

1. What is your father's / mother's job?
2. Where does he / she work?
3. What does he / she do?
4. How long has he / she worked there?
5. Does he / she like his / her job?
6. What doesn't he / she like about the job?

7. Would you like to have the same job as your father? Why?
8. Would you like to have the same job as your mother? Why?
9. What are some indoor jobs?
10. Which indoor jobs do you like? Why?
11. Which indoor jobs do you dislike? Why?
12. What are some outdoor jobs?
13. Which outdoor jobs do you like? Why?
14. Which outdoor jobs do you dislike? Why?

Grammar Focus: Fill in the blanks.

Freddy _____ a high school teacher. He _____ math and P.E. (physical

education) at Carver High School. He _____ his job very much. He _____

worked there for ten years. In math class Freddy _____ algebra to his

students. In PE class Freddy and his students _____ different kinds of sports.

He _____ working with high school students but sometimes the job ___

tiring and he _____ tired.

Marcia _____ a sales representative. She _____ in an office. She _____

worked there for seven years. She _____ watches to department stores and

to boutiques. She _____ on the telephone and _____ with her customers.

She _____ her job very much, however sometimes her throat _____ sore

because she has to _____ a lot.

Lesson 4 — Food and Beverages

Look at these pictures. Say something about each.

John and Maria are meeting for lunch.

John and Maria are in the University food court. The food court has many different choices for students when they are hungry. There are many different kinds of food stalls in the food court. There are sandwich stalls. There are salad stalls. There are pizza stalls, hamburger stalls, and chicken stalls too. There are also many different kinds of international food stalls. There is Chinese food, Japanese food, Thai food, Indian food, and Mexican food.

There are also many different kinds of beverages for students to choose when they are thirsty. They can choose soda, tea, coffee, milk, mineral water, or juice. They can buy beverages from a food stall or from a vending machine. The vending machines also sell snacks, like potato chips or cookies.

Students can choose many different kinds of food and drink for breakfast, lunch, dinner, or just a snack. They eat breakfast in the morning. They eat lunch at noon. They eat dinner in the evening. They eat a snack anytime. Today, John and Maria will have lunch together. They are talking about the different kinds of food they like and dislike.

Dialogue: Maria and John are talking about food.

John: *Hi Maria, how are you doing?*
Maria: *I'm fine John, how about you?*
John: *Actually, I'm hungry.*
Maria: *Well, you came to the right place. There are many things to eat here.*
John: *I know. But there are so many choices that I don't know what to choose.*
Maria: *Well, what kind of food do you like?*
John: *I like pizza **and** salad, **but** I don't like hamburgers **or** sandwiches.*
Maria: *OK, why don't you have pizza and salad?*
John: *But I had that yesterday.*
Maria: *Maybe you can try one of the international foods they have here.*
John: *What do you suggest?*
Maria: *Well, I like Chinese **and** Japanese food, **but** I don't like Mexican **or** Indian food.*
John: *Why don't you like Mexican or Indian food?*
Maria: *They are too spicy for me.*
John: *Oh, I see. I like spicy food.*
Maria: *Then maybe you can choose Mexican or Indian food for lunch today.*
John: *That's a good idea Maria. I think I'll have some tacos. How about you?*
Maria: *I think I'll have a slice of pizza and some salad today.*
John: *That sounds like a good idea. Let's hurry up, I'm starving.*
Maria: *Me too. Talking about food always makes me hungrier!*

Questions:

1. Where are John and Maria?
2. What can students buy in the food court?
3. What kind of international food can students buy?
4. Where can students buy beverages?
5. What do the vending machines sell?
6. When do people usually eat breakfast? Lunch? Dinner? Snacks?

7. How does John feel?
8. What does John like?
9. What doesn't he like?
10. What did he have for lunch yesterday?
11. What does Maria like?
12. What doesn't she like?

13. Does John like spicy food?
14. What does John decide to have?
15. What will Maria have?
16. What makes Maria hungrier?

Activity: Food Chart

Fill in the chart with some food and beverages you like and dislike.

Food I like	Food I dislike	Drinks I like	Drinks I dislike

Fill in the chart with different kinds of food and beverages your classmate likes and dislikes.

Food _____ likes	Food _____ dislikes	Drinks _____ likes	Drinks _____ dislikes

Discussion Questions:

1. Do you like sandwiches? What kind do you like?
2. Do you like salad? What kind?
3. Do you like pizza? What kind?
4. Do you like hamburgers? What American fast food do you like?
5. Have you ever had any international food? What kind? Where
6. What is your favorite kind of food? What is your favorite dish?
7. What food do you dislike? Why don't you like it?
8. What kind of beverages do you like? Where do you usually drink them?
9. What kind of beverages do you dislike? Why don't you like them?

10. What do you usually have for breakfast? Where?
11. What do you usually have for lunch? Where do you usually have lunch?
12. What do you usually have for dinner? Where do you usually have dinner?
13. What do you usually have for a snack? Where do you usually have it?
14. Can you cook? Who usually cooks for you and your family?
15. Do you know anyone who is a vegetarian? Tell us about him or her.

Grammar Focus: Sentence pattern: and / but / or.

Write about yourself:

I like to eat _____ **and** _____ , **but** I don't like to eat

_____ **or** _____.

I like to drink _____ **and** _____ , **but** I don't like to drink

_____ **or** _____.

Now write about your classmate:

_____ likes to eat _____ **and** _____ , **but** _____

doesn't like to eat _____ **or** _____.

_____ likes to drink _____ **and** _____ , **but** _____

doesn't like to drink _____ **or** _____.

Lesson 5	**Where do you live?**

Look at these pictures. Say something about them.

Patrick lives in a house. Kathy lives in an apartment.

- Patrick lives in a house. He lives with his wife and their two children. Their house has two floors. On the first floor there is a living room, a dining room, a kitchen, and a bathroom. On the second floor there are four bedrooms. Patrick and his wife sleep in the master bedroom and their children each have a bedroom. There is also a guest bedroom for visitors. On the second floor there are two bathrooms. One is for the children to use and one is in the master bedroom for Patrick and his wife. Their house also has a basement and a garage. They put things they don't use in the basement. They park their car in the garage. Patrick's house also has a front yard and a back yard for the children to play in.

- Kathy lives alone in an apartment. Her apartment is in an apartment building. The building has twelve floors. Kathy lives on the tenth floor. Her apartment has two bedrooms. One is for her and the other is a guest room. Her apartment also has a kitchen, a bathroom and a living room. The living room has a balcony with a good view. In the basement of the building there is a parking garage. All the people who live in the building can park their cars there. There is a garden on the roof of the building. The garden has many kinds of flowers and plants for the residents to enjoy.

Dialogue: Patrick and Kathy are talking about where they live.

Patrick: *Hi Kathy, how are you doing?*
Kathy: *Not bad, how about you Patrick?*
Patrick: *I'm fine, thanks. How is the new apartment?*
Kathy: *It's ok. It's comfortable for one person.*
Patrick: *How many rooms does it have?*
Kathy: *It has five rooms. There are two bedrooms a bathroom, a kitchen, and a living room.*
Patrick: *It sounds like a nice place.*
Kathy: *Yes, I think I will be happy there.*
Patrick: *We want to re-decorate our house.*
Kathy: *Why do you want to do that?*
Patrick: *Well, the wallpaper in the living room is getting old.*
Kathy: *So you would like to change it?*
Patrick: *That's right. And we would also like to paint the bedrooms.*
Kathy: *How many bedrooms do you have?*
Patrick: *There are four bedrooms in our house. One master bedroom, two for the children and a guest room.*
Kathy: *It sounds like you will need a lot of paint!*

Questions:

1. Where does Patrick live?
2. How many floors are there?
3. Which rooms are on the first floor?
4. Which rooms are on the second floor?
5. How many bedrooms are there?
6. Which bedroom does Patrick sleep in?
7. How many bathrooms are in his house?
8. What else is in his house?
9. Where do the children play?
10. What does Patrick want to do?
11. Why does he want to change?
12. Why will he need a lot of paint?

13. Where does Kathy live now?
14. How many floors are in the building?
15. What floor does she live on?
16. How many rooms are there?
17. What rooms are they?
18. What else does her apartment have?
19. What is in the roof garden?
20. Who can enjoy the roof garden?

Activity: Furniture

Write some furniture and other things you would usually see in each room.

Bedroom	Living room	Bathroom	Kitchen
Bed...	*Couch...*		

Now, ask your classmates if they have any of the furniture that you put on your list in the rooms in their house or apartment.

Ask: *Do you have a _____ in your _____?*

Example: *Do you have a bed in your bedroom?*
Classmate answers: *Yes, I do.* Or *No, I don't.*

Discussion Questions:

1. Do you live in a house or in an apartment?
2. Have you always lived there?
3. How many floors are there?
4. How many bedrooms are there?
5. How many bathrooms are there?
6. What is in the living room?
7. What is in the kitchen?
8. Are there any other rooms? What are they?
9. Are there any balconies? How many?

10. Do you have a garden? What is in it?
11. What color are the walls inside?
12. What color is the outside?
13. Do you know your neighbors? What are they like? How often do you see them?
14. Which is your favorite room? Why?
15. Do you like where you live? Why?

16. If you could change something about where you live, what would you change?

I would like to change the _____

Grammar Focus: Fill in the blanks.

Patrick lives in a _____. He _____ with his wife and their two

children. Their house has two _____. On the _____ floor there is

a living room, a dining room, a kitchen and a _____. On the

_____ floor there are four bedrooms. Patrick and his wife sleep in the

_____ _____ and their children each _____ a bedroom.

There is also a guest bedroom for _____.

Lesson 6	Colors

Use a marker to draw the colors in the space.

Red

Blue

Green

Orange

Purple

White

Black

Yellow

Pink

Marcia has moved into a new house.

Marcia's new house is very colorful. The living room has beige walls. There are 2 dark green chairs and there is a dark green sofa with a table in front of it. There are flowers on the table and paintings on the walls. The flowers are red. There are plants next to the windows. The plants are green. There is a table in the kitchen and there are 4 chairs around the table. The table and chairs are brown. There are brown cupboards in the kitchen and the walls are orange. There are 2 windows but there aren't any plants next to them. There is a sink, toilet, and bathtub in the bathroom. There isn't a shower and there aren't any windows. The walls are red.

Marcia's bedroom is very big. The walls are light blue and there is a big bed with a navy blue armchair next to the bed. There is a large closet in her bedroom. She puts her clothes in the closet. She has a large desk in her bedroom with her computer on it. There are 2 tables and 2 windows. There is a telephone on one table and a television on the other table. The telephone is black and the table is white. There are some small trees next to the windows but there aren't any flowers.

There are a lot of trees, plants, and flowers in her yard. There is a swimming pool but there isn't a garden. Marcia is very happy with her new house.

Dialogue: Marcia and her mom are talking about her new house.

Marcia: *Hi Mom. What a pleasant surprise.*
Linda: *Well, I was in the neighborhood and I thought I'd stop by.*
Marcia: *Come on in.*
Linda: *Gee Marcia, the place looks great.*
Marcia: *Thanks Mom. It was a lot of hard work but it's all finished now.*
Linda: *That's a nice sofa. I love dark green. Where did you buy it?*
Marcia: *There is a furniture store on Main Street. I bought it there.*
Linda: *Isn't there a furniture store on Brown Street?*
Marcia: *No, there isn't. That store closed last year.*
Linda: *Are there any red sofas at the store on Main Street?*
Marcia: *There aren't any red sofas but there are black, blue, and purple sofas.*
Linda: *Maybe I'll go over there sometime. I want a new sofa for my living room.*
Marcia: *Come and look at my kitchen. I painted it orange.*
Linda: *Eeek! There's a spider!*
Marcia: *Oh Mom. That isn't a real spider. That is Rover's toy spider.*
Linda: *There aren't any spiders but there are ants. Look over there.*
Marcia: *Oh no. I just cleaned the kitchen a few minutes ago.*
Linda: *Looks like you have more work to do.*

Questions:

1. How many rooms does Marcia's house have?
2. Does she have a yard?
3. What color are the walls in her living room?
4. Are there any pictures on the walls?
5. Is there a television in the kitchen?
6. Where are the chairs in the kitchen?
7. Is there a computer in the bedroom?
8. Is there a closet in the bedroom?
9. Are there any windows in the bathroom?
10. What does Linda think about Marcia's house?
11. What color is Marcia's sofa?
12. Where did Marcia buy the sofa?
13. Is there a furniture shop on Brown Street?
14. Is there a spider in Marcia's kitchen?
15. Who is Rover?
16. Are there any cockroaches in Marcia's kitchen?
17. What did Marcia do a few minutes ago?

Activity: Describing Your House

Describe your house or apartment.

How many	Colors	Things in there
Floors		
Bedrooms		
Bathrooms		
Living rooms		
Dining rooms		
Closets		
Balconies		
Gardens		

Now, ask a classmate to describe his or her house or apartment.

How many	Colors	Things in there
Floors		
Bedrooms		
Bathrooms		
Living rooms		
Dining rooms		
Closets		
Balconies		
Gardens		

Discussion Questions:

1. Do you live in a house or in an apartment?
2. What color are the living room walls?
3. What color are the kitchen walls?
4. What colors are your bedroom walls?
5. What color is your car?
6. What color is your hair?
7. What color is chocolate?
8. What color is the sun? What things are yellow?
9. What color are carrots? What things are orange?
10. What color are apples? What things are green?
11. What color is snow? What things are white?
12. What are you wearing today? What color is it?
13. What is your favorite color?
14. Which colors don't you like?

Grammar Focus.

Put the words in the correct order to make questions about houses.

1. bedroom / is / color / What / your

   _____?

2. plants / Are / in / your / any / there / bathroom

   _____?

3. kitchen / there / your / Are / pictures /any / in

   _____?

4. color / What / living room / is / your

   _____?

Answer the questions using yes *there is / are,* **or** *no there is / are not.*

1. Are there any ants in your kitchen? _____

2. Is there a telephone in your living room? _____

3. Are there any paintings in your bathroom? _____

4. Is there a table in your bedroom? _____

Lesson 7	**School**

Look at these pictures. Say something about them.

Maria and John are schoolmates at the university.

Maria is a student at the state university. She is studying business. She likes university, but the work is very hard. She likes to study and to learn about business. Maria has always liked going to school. In kindergarten Maria liked to draw pictures. In elementary school she liked to learn about American history. In junior high school she liked to learn math. In high school her favorite subjects were English and math, but she didn't like to study history or science. Maria is a good student. She always does her homework and always gets good grades.

John is a state university student also. He is studying computer science. He likes to go to university, but the work is difficult and he has to study very hard. John has always liked going to school, too. In kindergarten John liked to sing songs. In elementary school he liked to read books. In junior high school he liked to learn math, also. In high school his favorite subjects were history and science but he didn't like to study English or math. John is a good student too, but sometimes he is a little lazy. Sometimes he doesn't study hard enough.

Dialogue: Maria and John are talking about school.

Maria: *Hi John.*
John: *Hi Maria, how is school?*
Maria: *Pretty good, but I'm very busy right now.*
John: *Why are you so busy?*
Maria: *I have to do a report before next Friday.*
John: *I'm pretty busy, too.*
Maria: *Why are you busy?*
John: *I have to study for mid-term exams.*
Maria: *When are your exams?*
John: *They begin next Monday and finish on Friday.*
Maria: *How many exams do you have?*
John: *I have five exams. One in each subject.*
Maria: *Well, study hard and good luck.*
John: *Thanks, Maria. Good luck with your report.*
Maria: *Thanks, John.*

Questions:

1. Where do Maria and John study?
2. What does Maria study?
3. What does John study?
4. What did Maria like in kindergarten?
5. What did she like in elementary school?
6. What did she like in junior high school?
7. What were Maria's favorite subjects in high school?
8. What subjects didn't Maria like in high school?

9. What did John like in kindergarten?
10. What did he like in elementary school?
11. What did he like in junior high school?
12. What were John's favorite subjects in high school?
13. What subjects didn't John like in high school?

14. Is Maria a good student?
15. Is John a good student?
16. Why is Maria busy?
17. Why is John busy?

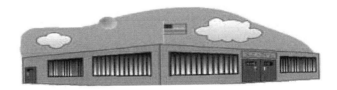

Activity: School Chart

Fill in this chart with subjects you liked and disliked in school.

School	Liked	Disliked
Elementary		
Junior High		
Senior High		
College / University		
Cram		

Ask your classmate: *What did you like to learn in (elementary school)   ?*

Classmate answers: *I liked to learn _____ in elementary school.*

Fill in this chart with subjects your classmate liked and disliked.

School	Liked	Disliked
Elementary		
Junior High		
Senior High		
College / University		
Cram		

Discussion Questions:

1. Did you go to elementary school? Where?
2. Which subjects did you like in elementary school? Why?
3. Which subjects didn't you like in elementary school? Why?
4. Did you get good grades in elementary school?
5. Did you always do your homework in elementary school?

6. Did you go to junior high school? Where?
7. Which subjects did you like in junior high school? Why?
8. Which subjects didn't you like in junior high school? Why?
9. Did you get good grades in junior high school?
10. Did you always do your homework in junior high school?

11. Did you go to college or university? Where?
12. Which subjects did you like in college? Why?
13. Which subjects didn't you like in college? Why?

14. Which cram schools have you been to?
15. What did you learn at cram school? Did you like to study there?

Grammar Focus: Fill in the blanks.

Maria is a _____ at the state university. She is _____ business. She

likes university, but the work is very _____. She likes to study and to _____

about business. In _____ Maria liked to draw pictures. In

_____ _____ she liked to learn about American history. In _____

_____ _____ she liked to learn math. In _____ _____ her favorite

subjects were English and math, but she didn't like to study history or science.

Maria is a good student. She always does her _____ and she always

gets good _____.

Lesson 8 — How was your day today?

Look at these pictures. Say something about them.

Charles usually does the same thing everyday.

Charles wakes up at six o'clock every morning from Monday to Friday. He gets up, takes a shower, gets dressed, and eats breakfast. He usually has coffee and cereal for breakfast. Sometimes he has toast and juice. He never has tea or eggs for breakfast. He doesn't like them.

At 7:15 Charles leaves for work. He always drives to work. Charles works in a bank. He is the bank manager. He is always busy in the morning. He usually has a meeting with his staff. He sometimes talks to customers on the phone. He is always in a good mood at work. He is never grumpy.

Charles usually works until five o'clock. Sometimes he works overtime and finishes at six o'clock. He never goes home early. After work, Charles goes home. At home he always has dinner with his wife Susan and their two children. After dinner, Charles and his wife usually watch television and their children do their homework. Sometimes the children finish their homework early. Then, the family will watch TV together. They usually watch a movie. They never watch soap operas.

The children usually go to bed at ten o'clock. Before they go to bed they always brush their teeth and wash their hands and face. Charles and his wife usually go to bed at eleven o'clock.

Dialogue: Charles and Susan are talking after dinner.

Susan: *How was your day today?*
Charles: *Very good, thanks.*
Susan: *Do you have to work overtime this week?*
Charles: *I'm not sure. Probably not.*
Susan: *That's good. Then you can come home earlier.*
Charles: *What are the children doing?*
Susan: *They're doing their homework, as usual.*
Charles: *They always do their homework after dinner.*
Susan: *Do you want to watch TV?*
Charles: *Not right now. I have a little work to do.*
Susan: *Are you going upstairs?*
Charles: *No, I'll work in the dining room.*
Susan: *I'm going to see if the kids need any help with their homework.*
Charles: *OK. I hope you can help them.*
Susan: *I hope they don't need help with math. My math is not good.*
Charles: *I'll help them with math. You help them with English.*
Susan: *OK. It's a deal.*

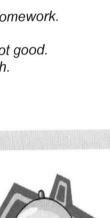

Questions:

1. What time does Charles usually get up?
2. What does he do after he gets up?
3. What does he usually have for breakfast?
4. What does he never have for breakfast?

5. What time does he leave for work?
6. How does he get to work?
7. What does Charles do?
8. How is his mood at work?

9. What time does he usually finish work?
10. What does he do after work?
11. What does he do at home?
12. What does the family do after dinner?
13. What do they usually watch on TV?
14. What do they never watch on TV?

15. What time do the children usually go to bed?
16. What do they do before they go to bed?
17. What time do Charles and his wife go to bed?

Activity: How Often Do You ...?

How often do you do these activities? Check the right box.

Activity	Always	Usually	Sometimes	Never
Have milk for breakfast				
Have lunch at home				
Exercise				
Take a nap				
Read the newspaper				
Go to see a movie				
Chat on the phone				
Be late for class				
Be early for class				
Do housework				

Ask your classmate: *How often do you do these activities?*

Activity	Always	Usually	Sometimes	Never
Have milk for breakfast				
Have lunch at home				
Exercise				
Take a nap				
Read the newspaper				
Go to see a movie				
Chat on the phone				
Be late for class				
Be early for class				
Do housework				

Discussion Questions:

1. What time do you usually get up?
2. Do you always get up at the same time?
3. How do you usually get up? Do you have an alarm clock?
4. What do you usually do after you get up?
5. What do you usually have for breakfast?
6. What time do you usually leave for work or school?
7. How do you usually get to work or school?
8. What do you usually do when you get there?
9. What time do you usually finish work or school?
10. What do you usually do after work or school?

11. What do you usually do when you first get home?
12. What does your family usually do after dinner?
13. What time do you usually go to bed?
14. What do you usually do before you go to bed?
15. Which days do you usually have off?
16. What do you usually do on these days?
17. What do you never do on your days off?
18. Are you ever late to work?
19. What other things are you late for?
20. Are you ever early for something? What?

Grammar Focus: Which one is correct?

Charles wakes up at six o'clock every morning.
Charles wake up at six o'clock every morning.

He usually have coffee and cereal for breakfast.
He usually has coffee and cereal for breakfast.

Charles works in a bank. He has worked there for 20 years.
Charles works in a bank. He have worked there for 20 years.

At home Charles has dinner with his wife Susan and there two children.
At home Charles has dinner with his wife Susan and their two children.

Charles usually works from Monday to Friday every week.
Charles usually work from Monday to Friday every week.

He always has Saturday and Sunday off.   She don't work tomorrow.
He always have Saturday and Sunday off.   She doesn't work tomorrow.

Charles very likes to play golf.   He very enjoys playing golf.
Charles really likes to play golf.   He enjoys playing golf very much.

Lesson 9　　　Is Freddy there?

Look at these pictures. Say something about them.

John's telephone is ringing.

"Hi, this is John. I can't come to the phone right now. Please leave your name and number after the beep and I'll get back to you as soon as I can."

John isn't at home right now. Someone is calling him and they are hearing John's voice on an answering machine. The person may leave a message after he or she hears a beep. Some people don't like to leave messages. They just hang up when they hear an answering machine. Answering machines are very useful. People have them in their home or in their offices. They can record messages when they are not able to answer the telephone. Freddy listened to John's answering machine and then he left a message.

"Hi John, this is Freddy. I really enjoyed playing Mah Jong last weekend. Can we play again this weekend? Give me a call when you have time. My home number is 633-7758. My cell phone number is 0946823419. See you later."

John got home at 7:30. He listened to Freddy's message. Now, John is calling Freddy back.

Dialogue: Freddy and John are talking on the telephone.

Freddy: *Hello.*
John: *Is Freddy there?*
Freddy: *This is Freddy.*
John: *Hi Freddy. It's John.*
Freddy: *John thanks for calling me back.*
John: *No problem. So, you liked playing Mah Jong last weekend?*
Freddy: *Yeah, that was a lot of fun. Can you play again this weekend?*
John: *Sorry, I can't. This weekend I have to study for my final exams.*
Freddy: *Oh, I understand. Final exams are very important.*
John: *How about next weekend? I'll have a lot of free time after my exams.*
Freddy: *That sounds great.*
John: *Where do you want to play?*
Freddy: *How about my house?*
John: *Sure. What's your address?*
Freddy: *I live at 733 Merrill Avenue. Do you know where that is?*
John: *I know where that is.*
Freddy: *Is 7:00 okay?*
John: *Sounds good. You know Freddy sometimes we play Mah Jong for money.*
Freddy: *Maybe I'll gamble after I play a few more times.*
John: *Okay, that's fair. See you next Saturday.*

Questions:

1. Who is calling John?
2. What does he want?
3. Does Freddy leave his address in the message?
4. What is Freddy's home phone number?
5. When does Freddy want to play Mah Jong?
6. Does John call Freddy back?
7. What is Freddy's cell phone number?
8. What did John and Freddy do last weekend?
9. How does Freddy feel about Mah Jong?
10. What does John have to do this weekend?
11. What will they do next weekend?
12. Where will John and Freddy play Mah Jong??
13. What is Freddy's address?
14. Does John know where Freddy lives?
15. What time will they play Mah Jong next weekend?
16. Will Freddy gamble next weekend?
17. When will Freddy gamble?

Activity: Weekends

Find out what your classmates did last weekend, are doing this weekend, and will do next weekend.

Name	Last Weekend	This Weekend	Next Weekend

Practice the following telephone dialogue with a classmate. Fill in the missing information.

A: *Is _____ there?*

B: *This is _____.*

A: *Hi _____. It's _____.*

B: *Hi _____.*

A: *Can you _____ this weekend?*

B: *Sorry, I can't _____ this weekend, I'm busy. How about next weekend?*

A: *Sure. Next weekend is fine.*

B: *Great! See you then.*

A: *Okay, bye.*

Discussion Questions:

1. What year is it this year? Last year? Next year?
2. What month is this month? Last month? Next month?
3. What did you do last weekend?
4. What are you planning to do next weekend? Next month? Next year?

5. What is your home telephone number?
6. What is your address?
7. Do you ever play Mah Jong?
8. Do you ever play cards?
9. Do you ever gamble?

10. Do you have an answering machine?
11. Do you like to leave messages on answering machines?
12. How often do you talk on the telephone?
13. Who do you talk to? What do you talk about?
14. Do you have a cell-phone? What is the number?
15. Do you thinks cell-phones are useful? Why?

Grammar Focus.

Write the correct word: Next, this, or last.

1. _____ weekend we went to the mountains.

2. _____ Tuesday we are going to Tokyo.

3. We went to Disneyland _____ year.

4. Are you going to America _____ month?

5. I forgot my book _____week.

6. _____ week we will have a test.

7. He's going to work _____ morning.

8. He will come home _____ afternoon.

9. Do you have any plans for _____ weekend?

10. Where did you go _____ month?

Lesson 10   **Weekly Schedules**

Look at these pictures. Say something about them.

Anita and Marcia have busy schedules.

Anita is a housewife. She is always busy. On Mondays she buys groceries. On Tuesdays she does the laundry. On Wednesdays she does gardening and cleans outside the house. On Thursdays she runs errands. On Fridays she goes to yoga class. On Saturdays she usually helps her children with their homework and then they all go out to eat. They like to go to an Italian restaurant. On Sundays the family usually goes out for the day.

Marcia is a sales representative. She is usually busy, too. She works from Monday to Friday. After work on Mondays she goes to the gym. She does aerobics there. On Tuesdays she usually goes to the supermarket. She buys groceries at the supermarket. On Wednesdays she usually watches her favorite television shows. She likes to watch evening soap operas. On Thursdays she goes on-line. She likes to look at fashion and travel websites. On Fridays she likes to take a long bath and read a novel. Marcia is engaged. On Saturdays she and her fiancé like to go out to eat. They like to go to a seafood restaurant. On Sundays she and her fiancé like to take a drive.

Dialogue: Anita and Marcia are chatting.

Anita: *Hi Marcia, how are you?*
Marcia: *Fine, thanks Anita. How are you?*
Anita: *I'm fine. What are you going to do this week?*
Marcia: *On Monday I'm going to work and then I'm going to the gym.*
Anita: *What do you do at the gym?*
Marcia: *I do aerobics.*
Anita: *What are you going to do on Tuesday?*
Marcia: *After work I'm going grocery shopping.*
Anita: *What are you going to do on Wednesday?*
Marcia: *After work, I'm going to stay
                home and watch TV.*
Anita: *What are you going to do on Thursday?*
Marcia: *I want to check some travel information.*
Anita: *Are you going on vacation this year?*
Marcia: *Yes. I'm planning to go to Egypt.*
Anita: *Egypt? That sounds exciting.*
Marcia: *Yes, I think so too.*
Anita: *What are you going to do on the weekend?*
Marcia: *On Friday I'm going to take a bath and read
                a novel. On Saturday and Sunday I'm going to go out with my fiancé.*

**Write the seven
days of the week**

_____

_____

_____

_____

_____

_____

_____

Questions:

1.   What does Anita do on Mondays?
2.   What does she do on Tuesdays?
3.   What does she do on Wednesdays?
4.   What does she do on Thursdays?
5.   What does she do on Fridays?
6.   What does she do on Saturday?
7.   What does she do on Sundays?

8.   What does Marcia do on Mondays?
9.   What does she do on Tuesdays?
10. What does she do on Wednesdays?
11. What does she do on Thursdays?
12. What does she do on Fridays?
13. What does she do on Saturdays?
14. What does she do on Sundays?
15. What will Marcia do on Thursday?
16. Where is she planning to go this year?
17. What does Anita think about Marcia's plans?

What day is...

- **Before Tuesday?**
- **Before Thursday?**
- **Before Saturday?**
- **Before Sunday?**
- **Before Wednesday?**
- **Before Friday?**
- **Before Monday?**

- **After Tuesday?**
- **After Friday?**
- **After Thursday?**
- **After Sunday?**
- **After Wednesday?**
- **After Monday?**
- **After Saturday?**

Activity: Weekly Routines

In the chart write down what you usually do on each day of the week. Write two or three activities for each day.

Day of the week	What do you usually do?
Monday	
Tuesday	
Wednesday	
Thursday	
Friday	
Saturday	
Sunday	

In this chart write down what your classmate usually does.

Day of the week	What do you usually do?
Monday	
Tuesday	
Wednesday	
Thursday	
Friday	
Saturday	
Sunday	

Discussion Questions:

1. What do you usually do on Mondays?
2. What do you usually do on Tuesdays
3. What do you usually do on Wednesdays
4. What do you usually do on Thursdays?
5. What do you usually do on Fridays?
6. What do you usually do on Saturdays?
7. What do you usually do on Sundays?

8. Which is your favorite day of the week? Why?
9. Which is your least favorite day of the week? Why?
10. Who usually buys groceries for your family? Where?
11. Who usually cooks dinner for your family? What?
12. What do you and your family usually do on weekends?
13. Do you ever do yoga? Do you ever do aerobics?
14. What exercise do you like to do?

15. How often do you watch TV? Which TV shows do you like to watch?
16. Do you like to go out to eat? Where do you like to go?
17. Do you ever go on-line? What kind of websites do you like to look at?
18. Which do you prefer: taking shower or taking a bath? Why?
19. Do you and your family ever go out for the day? Where do you go?
20. Which places near where you live are good to go for a day out?

Grammar Focus: Fill in the blanks.

Marcia ____a sales representative. She is usually busy, too. She _____ from

Monday to Friday. After work on Mondays she _____ to the gym. She

_____aerobics there. On Tuesdays she usually _____ to the supermarket.

She _____ groceries at the supermarket. On Wednesdays she usually

_____her favorite television shows. She _____ to watch evening soap

operas. On Thursdays she _____on-line. She _____ to look at fashion and

travel websites. On Fridays she likes to _____ a long bath and read

a _____. Marcia is _____. On Saturdays she goes out with her

_____. On Sundays she and _____ fiancé like to _____a drive.

Lesson 11 — How was your weekend?

Look at these pictures. Say something about them.

Read about Freddy's weekend.

Freddy likes weekends. On Saturdays he likes to sleep late. He usually wakes up at nine o'clock on Saturday mornings. After he wakes up he makes breakfast and drinks a cup of coffee. On Saturday afternoons he goes to the park and plays basketball with his friends. On Saturday evenings he usually goes out with his girlfriend. They go out to dinner and then sometimes go to see a movie. Freddy goes to bed late on Saturday nights. He usually goes to bed at midnight.

On Sundays Freddy also sleeps late. He usually wakes up at nine thirty on Sunday mornings. After he wakes up, Freddy makes breakfast. After breakfast he usually listens to music to relax. He likes jazz music. On Sunday afternoons Freddy usually reads the newspaper. He likes to read the Sunday paper. Sometimes he reads a magazine or a novel. He likes to read sports magazines and police novels. Freddy also likes to cook. Every Sunday evening he makes dinner for his girlfriend. Freddy is a romantic guy.

On Sunday nights Freddy watches TV and goes to bed early. He usually goes to bed at ten o'clock, because the next day is Monday and he has to go to work. Freddy doesn't like Mondays, but he likes Fridays. Freddy always says, "Thank God it's Friday" on Fridays because the next day is Saturday. Then, he can relax and enjoy the weekend.

Dialogue: Freddy's co-worker Jane is asking him about his weekend.

Jane: *Hi Freddy. How was your weekend?*
Freddy: *Very good, thank you.*
Jane: *What did you do?*
Freddy: *Well, on Saturday morning I got up late and then made breakfast.*
Jane: *What did you do on Saturday afternoon?*
Freddy: *I went to the park and played basketball with my friends.*
Jane: *What did you do on Saturday night?*
Freddy: *My girlfriend and I went out to dinner and then we saw a movie.*
Jane: *That sounds like fun. What did you do on Sunday?*
Freddy: *On Sunday morning I listened to some music.*
Jane: *What did you do on Sunday afternoon?*
Freddy: *On Sunday afternoon I read a novel.*
Jane: *What did you do on Sunday evening?*
Freddy: *On Sunday evening I cooked dinner for my girlfriend.*
Jane: *What did you cook?*
Freddy: *I cooked fish, vegetables and rice. We also drank some white wine.*
Jane: *It sounds like you had a good weekend.*
Freddy: *Yes, I did. How about you? How was your weekend?*
Jane: *My weekend was pretty boring. I just stayed home and watched TV.*
Freddy: *Yes, that is pretty boring. I seldom watch TV on the weekends.*

Questions:

1. When does Freddy get up on Saturdays?
2. What does he do on Saturday mornings?
3. What does he do on Saturday afternoons?
4. What does he do on Saturday evenings?
5. What does he do on Saturday nights?

6. When does Freddy get up on Sundays?
7. What does he do on Sunday mornings?
8. What does he do on Sunday afternoons?
9. What does he do on Sunday evenings?
10. What does he do on Sunday night?

11. What did he do on Saturday morning?
12. What did he do on Saturday afternoon?
13. What did he do on Saturday evening?
14. What did he do on Saturday night?

15. What did he do on Sunday morning?
16. What did he do on Sunday afternoon?
17. What did he do on Sunday evening?
18. What did he do on Sunday night?

Write the past tense.

Get _____

Go _____

See _____

Read _____

Drink _____

Is _____

Stay _____

Watch _____

Activity: A Fun Weekend

Plan a fun weekend for you and your friends or your family. Write a fun activity for each time of the day. Have fun!

Time of day:	Activity:
Saturday morning	
Saturday afternoon	
Saturday evening	
Saturday night	
Sunday morning	
Sunday afternoon	
Sunday evening	
Sunday night	

Ask your classmates about their fun weekend.

Ask: *What did you do on* _____ *?*

Make sure they answer in the past tense.

Discussion Questions:

1. What did you do last Friday night?
2. What did you do last Saturday?
3. What did you do last Sunday?
4. What will you do this Friday night?
5. What will you do this Saturday?
6. What will you do this Sunday?

7. Would you rather go out or stay home on the weekends? Why?
8. What do you usually do at home on the weekends?
9. What do you never do at home on the weekends?
10. Where do you sometimes go on the weekends?
11. Where do you never go on the weekends?
12. What do your family like to do on the weekends?
13. What do you usually have for dinner on Saturdays?
14. Do you ever go out to eat on the weekend? Where do you go? What do you have? Who do you go with?
15. What places are crowded on the weekends? Why do people go there?

Grammar Focus: Change to past tense.

Freddy _____ up at nine o'clock on Saturday morning. After he _____ up he _____ breakfast and _____ a cup of coffee. On Saturday afternoon he _____ to the park and _____ basketball with his friends. On Saturday evening he _____ _____ with his girlfriend. They _____ _____ to dinner and then _____ a movie. On Sunday morning he _____ to some music. On Sunday afternoon he _____ his new novel. On Sunday evening he _____ dinner for his girlfriend. He _____ fish, vegetables and rice and they _____ some white wine.

On Sunday night Freddy _____ to bed early. He _____ to bed at ten o'clock, because the next day he _____ to work.

Lesson 12   Summer Vacations

Look at these pictures. Say something about them.

John and Freddy are at the gym.

John and Freddy are at the gym. They are talking about their summer vacations. People like to do many different things during summer vacation. Some people take trips to different countries. Some people go sightseeing in their own city. Some people visit relatives and friends. Some people like to enjoy nature. Some people like to stay home and relax.

John did a lot over summer vacation. He went to an amusement park. He rode on the roller coaster and ate cotton candy. He went to a museum. He saw many beautiful paintings and sculptures. He visited his sister in Dallas, Texas. He took a trip to Las Vegas and won a lot of money. He won $500 in a casino.

Freddy also did a lot over summer vacation. He went to the beach with his friends. He went water skiing and played volleyball. He went to a jazz music festival. He also took a trip with his girlfriend. They went camping in the mountains for one week. They hiked, fished and made a campfire at night. They slept in a tent. Today, John and Freddy are talking about what they did during their summer vacations.

Dialogue: John and Freddy are talking about summer vacation.

John: *Hey, Freddy. Long time no see.*
Freddy: *Yeah. How was your summer vacation?*
John: *It was great!*
Freddy: *Really? What did you do?*
John: *I went to an amusement park and rode the roller coaster. It was exciting!*
Freddy: *That sounds like fun. Did you do anything else?*
John: *I also visited my sister. Then, I flew to Las Vegas and won $500.*
Freddy: *You must have had a great time. I wish I could say the same.*
John: *Didn't you enjoy your summer vacation Freddy?*
Freddy: *It was terrible.*
John: *Really? What happened?*
Freddy: *Well, I went to the beach and went water skiing.*
John: *Water skiing sounds great.*
Freddy: *It was, but I forgot to put on sunscreen and got sunburned.*
John: *Oh, that's too bad. Did you do anything else?*
Freddy: *Yeah. I went camping in the mountains with my girlfriend.*
John: *I love camping. Did you go hiking and make a campfire.*
Freddy: *Yes but mosquitoes bit us and it rained for three days.*
John: *That's awful. You should have checked the weather forecast.*
Freddy: *That is what my girlfriend said.*

Questions:

1. Where are John and Freddy?
2. What are they talking about?
3. What did John do at the amusement park?
4. What did he see in the museum?
5. Where does his sister live?
6. What did he do in Las Vegas?
7. How much money did he win?

8. Where did Freddy go with his friends?
9. What did he do at the beach?
10. Where did he go with his girlfriend?
11. What did they do at night?
12. Where did Freddy go water-skiing?
13. What did he forget to put on at the beach?
14. Did Freddy check the weather forecast?
15. What did Freddy's girlfriend say?

Activity: Vacations

Fill in the chart with these expressions.

It was great.   Awful.   Not bad.   Terrible.   It was fantastic.

Terrific.   Nothing to do.   Not too good.   Nothing special.

I had a wonderful time.   So-so.   Boring.   It was all right.

Enjoyed the vacation	The vacation was OK	Not a good vacation

Think about your last vacation. Fill in the chart.

Where did you go	What did you do and see	Did you enjoy it

Ask your classmates about their last vacation. Fill in the chart.

Where did they go	What did they do and see	Did they enjoy it

Discussion Questions:

1. How was your last vacation?
2. Where did you go?
3. What did you do and see?
4. When did you go there?
5. How long were you there?
6. What did you like the most?
7. Would you go back again?
8. Was there anything you did not like?
9. Who did you go with?

10. Do you like taking long vacations or short vacations?
11. Have you ever gone on vacation by yourself? Where did you go?
12. Do you like staying home on vacation or going away?
13. What was your favorite vacation? Why?
14. When is your next vacation?
15. What will you do during your next vacation?
16. What won't you do during your next vacation?
17. When is the best time to take a vacation? Why?

Grammar Focus: Change these sentences into past tense.

1. I go on vacation to Hawaii. _____

2. I see many volcanoes. _____

3. They are amazing. _____

4. I go swimming in the ocean. _____

5. We take many pictures. _____

6. I go to go the beach everyday. _____

7. We go shopping. _____

8. Water skiing is fun. _____

9. We go on a sightseeing tour. _____

10. We have a wonderful vacation _____

Lesson 13 — Grocery Shopping

Look at these pictures. Say something about them.

Charles is going to the supermarket.

Charles is looking in his refrigerator. A refrigerator is often called a 'fridge' for short. People put things that need to stay cold in the refrigerator. Things that need to be frozen are put in the freezer. Charles has to go to the supermarket today so he is making a shopping list. People usually make a list of things to buy before they go to the store. If you make a list then you won't forget what to buy.

It has been a week since Charles went to the supermarket. There are only a few things in his refrigerator. There is a little milk and a little juice. There are a few eggs and a few apples. There is some cheese and some pasta noodles. There are a lot of onions and tomatoes but only one green pepper. There isn't any lettuce or garlic. There isn't any butter or bread either.

Charles is making dinner. He will start with a salad and then have spaghetti and meatballs with garlic bread for the main course. For dessert, he's making his famous apple pie with vanilla ice cream. His wife is excited because she doesn't have to cook tonight. She is helping him make a list for the supermarket.

Dialogue: Charles and his wife are making a list for the supermarket.

Charles: *Ok honey, what do I need to buy?*
Nancy: *Well, do we have enough noodles?*
Charles: *We have some noodles but not enough.*
Nancy: *How about tomato sauce?*
Charles: *I don't see any tomato sauce.*
Nancy: *Are there any onions?*
Charles: *Yes, we have a lot of onions.*
Nancy: *Do we need any tomatoes or garlic?*
Charles: *There are a lot of tomatoes but there isn't any garlic.*
Nancy: *Are you making a salad?*
Charles: *Yes I am, but there isn't any lettuce.*
Nancy: *Are there any apples for the pie?*
Charles: *There are a few apples. Maybe I'll buy a couple more.*
Nancy: *Did you look in the freezer for ice cream?*
Charles: *There isn't any vanilla but there is some chocolate ice cream.*
Nancy: *You should get vanilla ice cream. It goes best with apple pie.*
Charles: *So, I need some noodles, a can of tomato sauce, some garlic, a head of lettuce and a few apples. Is that everything?*
Nancy: *Don't forget bread and ice cream.*
Charles: *That's right, a carton of vanilla ice cream and a loaf of bread.*
Nancy: *One more thing. Don't forget your list.*
Charles: *Thanks for reminding me. Bye.*

Questions:

1. What is Charles doing?
2. Where is he going to go?
3. Why is he making a list?
4. Are there any oranges in his refrigerator?
5. Is there any bread?
6. Is there a lot of milk?
7. What is Charles making for dinner?
8. Is he making spaghetti?
9. What does Charles have to buy at the supermarket?

10. Will he buy any apples?
11. Will he buy a carton of ice cream?
12. What kind of ice cream will he buy?
13. How much bread will he buy?
14. What is Charles making for dessert?
15. What did Charles almost forget?

Activity: Grocery Charts

What is in your refrigerator right now? What is in your classmate's refrigerator right now?

Your refrigerator	Your classmate's

Cooking: Make a list of the things you would need for the following meals.

Green Salad with Corn Soup	Shrimp Fried Rice	Chicken Sandwich	Spaghetti with Garlic Bread

Discussion Questions:

1. Do you like to cook? Are you a good cook?
2. What is your favorite meal; breakfast, lunch, or dinner?
3. What is something that you always keep in your refrigerator?
4. What color is you refrigerator?
5. Do you often eat bread?
6. Do you usually eat everything in your fridge or do you throw a lot away?
7. Do you ever use mustard? Ketchup? Mayonnaise?
8. How often do you go to the supermarket? Outdoor market? Night market?
9. Do you ever make a shopping list? Why?

10. Do you put milk in the freezer or the refrigerator?
11. What kind of food do you keep in the freezer?
12. What do you keep in the crisper drawer?
13. Why do we need to keep food cold?
14. Have you ever smelled spoiled food? How does it smell?
15. How often do you clean out your fridge?

Grammar Focus.

Choose the correct word to finish the sentence:

1. There is (some / a few) ice cream.
2. Can I have (some / a few) bread?
3. There are (a little / few) apples.
4. Is there (a lot / some) of milk?
5. There is (some / a few) milk.
6. Charles has (a little / a few) apples.
7. I want (some / a few) juice.
8. She wants (a lot of / a few) soup.

 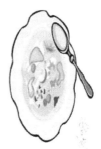

Correct the mistake in each sentence.

1. How many tomato sauce?

2. Are there much apple juice?

3. There isn't some bacon.

4. Are there any bread?

5. Does she have much sandwiches?

6. Would you like some a soup?

7. There is a few ice cream.

8. There isn't some butter.

9. Do we have many coffee?

10. There isn't some cheese.

11. I think I ate too many cake.

12. I don't drink many coffee.

Lesson 14   Shopping

Look at these pictures. Say something about them.

Anita and John are shopping for different things.

Anita is grocery shopping. She goes to the supermarket to buy groceries for her family. There are five people in her family, so she buys a lot of groceries every week. She buys meat, fish, bread, milk, rice, tea bags, coffee, cheese, cereal and cookies form the supermarket. The groceries cost $75.00. After the supermarket Anita goes to the outdoor market. She goes there because the fruit and vegetables are fresher. She buys lots of fruit and vegetables for her family. She spends $15.00 at the outdoor market. After the outdoor market Anita goes to the convenience store to buy some snacks for her family. The store is near her house. She spends $5.00 at the convenience store.

John needs to buy some school supplies. He goes to the stationery store. He buys 2 notebooks, some marker pens, an eraser and a plastic folder. He spends $10.00 at the stationery store. After the stationery store, John goes to the bookstore. He needs to buy a dictionary. He spends $7.00 at the bookstore. On the way home, John feels a little hungry and thirsty. He goes to the convenience store to buy a snack and a drink-box. He spends $3.00 at the convenience store.

Dialogue: Anita sees John at the convenience store.

Anita: *Hi John, how are you today?*
John: *I'm fine Anita, how about you?*
Anita: *I'm a little tired.*
John: *What have you been doing today?*
Anita: *I have been grocery shopping for my family.*
John: *Where did you go?*
Anita: *First I went to the supermarket, and then to the outdoor market.*
John: *I have been shopping, as well.*
Anita: *Have you been grocery shopping, too?*
John: *No, I have been buying some school supplies.*
Anita: *Where did you go?*
John: *Well, I needed some notebooks and pens, so I went to the stationery store. I also needed a dictionary, so I went to the bookstore.*
Anita: *What are you going to buy here?*
John: *I'm going to buy a snack and a drink-box. Shopping always makes me hungry and thirsty!*
Anita: *OK, John, have a good day.*
John: *You, too Anita. Goodbye.*

Questions:

1. What does Anita need?
2. Where does she go first?
3. What does she buy there?
4. How much does she spend?
5. Where does she go next?
6. What does she buy there?
7. How much does she spend?
8. Where does she go last?
9. What does she buy there?
10. How much does she spend in total?

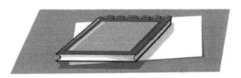

11. What does John need?
12. Where does he go first?
13. What does he buy there?
14. How much does he spend?
15. Where does he go next?
16. What does he buy there?
17. How much does he spend?
18. Where does he go last?
19. What does he buy there?
20. How much does he spend in total?

Activity: Shopping List

You are going shopping. Make a list of things to buy. They can be for you and your family or for your friends.

What do you need?	Where can you buy it?	How much will it cost?
A pair of shoes	*A shoe store*	*$ 40.00*

Practice with a classmate.

Ask: *Where are you going?*

Classmate answers: *I'm going to the* _____

Ask: *What are you going to buy?*

Classmate answers: *I'm going to buy* _____

Ask: *How much will it cost?*

Classmate answers: *It will cost* _____

Discussion Questions: Discuss these questions about shopping.

1. Do you like to go shopping?
2. Where do you usually go shopping?
3. What do you usually buy?
4. What was the last thing you bought at a department store?
5. About how much did it cost?
6. Why did you buy it?
7. What was the last thing you bought at a supermarket?
8. About how much did it cost?
9. Why did you buy it?

10. What was the last thing you bought at a convenience store?
11. About how much did it cost?
12. Why did you buy it?
13. What was the last thing you bought at a bookstore?
14. About how much did it cost?
15. Why did you buy it?
16. What was the last thing you bought from an outdoor market?
17. About how much did it cost?
18. Why did you buy it?

Grammar Focus: Sentence pattern.

When I need _____I go to the _____. It/they

will cost about _____.

When I need _____ I go to the _____. It/they

will cost about _____.

When I need _____ I go to the _____. It/they

will cost about _____.

Practice with a classmate:

1. **What do you need?**

   I need a/some _____.

2. **You should go to the _____store.**

3. **How much will it / they cost?**

   It / they will cost about _____ .

Lesson 15   What time do you wake up?

Look at these different times. Say them aloud.

Read about Patrick and Anita's schedules.

These are Patrick and Anita's schedules. Patrick is a restaurant owner. He works late at night. Anita is a housewife. She doesn't work but is still very busy. They have very different schedules. Patrick sleeps late. Anita wakes up early. Patrick has brunch at 12:00 but Anita has lunch at 12:00. Anita eats dinner at 5:00, but Patrick doesn't eat until 7:30.

Patrick usually wakes up around 10 or 11:00. He has brunch at 12:00. Brunch is a combination of breakfast and lunch. He always goes to softball practice at 1:30. Softball is his favorite sport. He goes to work at 4:00 to open the restaurant. Patrick is never late. At 7:30, Patrick goes home to eat dinner with his family. He goes back to work at 8:45. He usually finishes work by 2:30 a.m. He sometimes goes fishing with his friends after work but he usually goes home.

Anita wakes up very early.   She always goes to yoga class at 6:30 in the morning. At 7:45, she wakes the kids and makes them breakfast. Then, she takes the kids to school at 8:15. At 12:00, she has lunch with her friends from the gardening club. She picks the kids up at 3:45 and makes dinner at 5:00. Sometimes she goes to PTA meetings at night.

Dialogue: Patrick and Anita are talking about their schedules.

Anita: *Hey Patrick. How's the restaurant business?*
Patrick: *Not bad. I work a lot, but business is good.*
Anita: *So, you're busy these days?*
Patrick: *Yeah, I don't get home until 2:30 or 3:00 in the morning.*
Anita: *That's late. What time do you wake up?*
Patrick: *Usually around 10 or 11. How about you? What have you been doing lately?*
Anita: *I'm usually busy with the kids. They keep me very busy.*
Patrick: *Do you work?*
Anita: *No, I don't have time. I have to take the kids to school. Then I have to pick them up from school. Then I take them to piano lessons and baseball practice.*
Patrick: *Sounds like you are really busy.*
Anita: *I also go to yoga class in the morning and I'm still in the gardening club.*
Patrick: *Are you still a member of the PTA?*
Anita: *Yes, I am. There's a meeting tonight.*
Patrick: *Really? What time is the meeting?*
Anita: *The meeting is at a quarter after seven. Do you have time to go?*
Patrick: *Maybe. I'll check with my wife and see if she wants to go.*
Anita: *Great. Maybe I'll see you there.*
Patrick: *Ok Anita. Goodbye.*

Questions:

1. Does Anita wake up early or late?
2. When does Patrick eat brunch?
3. Does Patrick eat breakfast?
4. Why does Patrick go home at 7:30?
5. Does Patrick ever go fishing?
6. What time does Anita go to yoga class?
7. Do her kids go to yoga class with her?
8. When does Anita eat lunch?
9. Who does Anita eat lunch with?
10. What time does Anita pick up the kids?

11. What club is Anita in?
12. Are Anita and Patrick busy people?
13. Does Patrick work a lot?
14. What is Patrick's favorite sport?
15. How is business at Patrick's restaurant?
16. Will Patrick go to the PTA meeting?
17. When is the PTA meeting?

Activity: Daily Activities

Fill in the chart with your daily activities. Write down what you usually are doing at different times of the day.

Time of day	What do you usually do?
7:00 am	
11:30 am	
12:00 noon	
1:30 pm	
3:30 pm	
5:00 pm	
6:00 pm	
8:00 pm	
9:00 pm	
11:00 pm	

Now ask your classmate: *What do you usually do at*_____?

Your classmate should answer: *I usually* _____*at* _____.

What does your classmate usually do at …?	
7:30 AM	_____
1:30 PM	_____
9:45 PM	_____

Discussion Questions:

1. What time do you usually go to bed?
2. What time do you usually get up?
3. How many hours do you usually sleep every night?
4. Do you ever take a nap in the afternoon?
5. How many hours do you work or study in a day?
6. What time do you usually eat breakfast?
7. What time do you usually eat lunch?
8. What time do you usually eat dinner
9. What time does the sun rise?
10. What time does the sun set?

11. What time does the garbage truck come around your neighborhood?
12. What time is the TV news on?
13. What time is the best time to exercise?
14. What time is your favorite TV show on?
15. What time do other people in your family go to bed?
16. What time do they get up?
17. Who usually goes to bed first in your family?
18. Who usually gets up first in your family?
19. Do you use an alarm clock? What time do you set it for?

Grammar Focus: Write the different ways to say these times.

1. **3:15** _____

2. **4:45** _____

3. **1:20** _____

4. **9:40** _____

5. **10:05** _____

6. **7:30** _____

7. **11:45** _____

8. **12:15** _____

9. **10: 30** _____

10. **7: 11** _____

Lesson 16   Hobbies and Interests

Look at these pictures. Say something about each one.

Different people do different things in their free time.

There are many different activities you can do in your free time. Some people have a lot of free time and some do not. People like to spend their free time in many different ways. Today, Freddy, Charles, and Patrick are having dinner together. They are talking about what they like to do in their free time.

Charles enjoys playing golf and playing cards. He usually plays golf twice a month. He plays at a golf course in the countryside. He plays poker once every two weeks. He plays with some of his co-workers. They play in someone's house in the living room.

 Freddy likes playing basketball and going dancing. He plays basketball twice a week. He plays in the park with some of his friends. He goes dancing every Saturday night. He and his girlfriend go to a nightclub.

Patrick likes playing tennis and fishing with his kids. He usually plays tennis once or twice a week. He plays at a tennis court near his house. He usually plays with one of the people who work at his restaurant. Patrick also likes to go fishing with his kids. They usually go fishing once or twice a month. They go fishing in a river in the countryside.

Dialogue: Freddy, Charles, and Patrick are chatting about their free time.

Charles: *What do you like to do when you have free time, Patrick?*
Patrick: *I like fishing and playing tennis. Do you guys play tennis?*
Freddy: *Yes, but I don't play very often.*
Charles: *I usually try to play golf when I have free time.*
Freddy: *How often do you play golf?*
Charles: *I usually play once or twice a month. Sometimes I play three times a month. If I could, I would play everyday.*
Patrick: *Freddy, do you exercise in your free time?*
Freddy: *I sure do. I play basketball twice a week and I usually go dancing with my girlfriend on Saturday nights. What about you, Charles? What else do you do in your free time?*
Charles: *I like to play cards.*
Patrick: *How often do you play?*
Charles: *I usually play poker once every two weeks with friends from work.*
Freddy: *Hey, I thought of one more thing I like to do in my free time.*
Charles: *Oh, what's that?*
Freddy: *I love to eat in restaurants.*
Patrick: *I guess you're hungry again. I'll get you a menu.*

Questions:

1. What does Charles enjoy?
2. How often does he play golf?
3. Where does he play golf?
4. How often does he play poker?
5. Who does he play with?
6. Where do they play?

7. What does Freddy like to do?
8. How often does he play basketball?
9. Where does he play?
10. Who does he play with?
11. When does he go dancing?
12. Who does he go dancing with?
13. Where do they go?

14. What does Patrick like?
15. How often does he play tennis?
16. Where does he play?
17. Who does he play with?
18. What else does Patrick like to do?
19. How often do they go fishing?
20. Where do they go fishing?

Activity: Free Time Activities

Fill in the chart with different activities you like to do in your free time. Write how often you do them.

Free Time Activity	How Often

Fill in the chart with different activities your classmates like to do in their free time. Write how often they do them.

Classmate	Free Time Activity	How Often

Discussion Questions:

1. Would you rather...?

- Play golf or play cards? Why?
- Play basketball or play tennis? Why?
- Go dancing or go fishing? Why?

2. What do you like to do in your free time?
3. Do you have a lot of free time?
4. Do you wish you had more free time?
5. When do you have free time?
6. What things do you do everyday?
7. What do you do on Saturdays?
8. What do you do on Sundays?
9. What do you usually do in the evenings?

10. How often do you...?

Brush your teeth / Take a shower / Talk on the telephone / Take a bus / Drive a

car / Wash dishes / Cook dinner / Study English / See your parents / Watch TV?

Grammar Focus: Positive and negative sentences.

Make the positive sentences negative and the negative sentences positive.

Examples: **He likes to play soccer.** *He doesn't like to play soccer.*
Charles doesn't play golf. *Charles plays golf.*

1. Patrick doesn't play softball on Tuesdays. _____

2. I like going to movies. _____

3. Freddy has a lot of free time. _____

4. She doesn't like cooking. _____

5. He watches football on TV. _____

6. I don't like going out to eat. _____

7. Maria doesn't jog in the morning. _____

8. We listen to music a lot. _____

9. I don't have a lot of free time. _____

Lesson 17 — Last Week

Look at these pictures. Say something about each.

Anita was busy last week.

- On Monday she went shopping and bought groceries. She went to the supermarket and then to the outdoor market.

- On Tuesday she stayed at home. She did the laundry and did housework.

- On Wednesday she did some gardening and cleaned outside the house.

- On Thursday she went to the post office to buy some stamps and to send a package. Then, she went to the bank to deposit some money.

- On Friday she went to yoga class at the gym.

- On Saturday she helped her children with their homework and then they all went out to eat. They went to an Italian restaurant. Anita had spaghetti. Her husband had lasagna. The children had pizza.

- On Sunday the family went to the beach. At the beach Anita read a book. Her husband and the children played in the water. The weather was good. It was sunny and warm. When they went home that evening they were all tired, so they all went to bed early. The children went to bed at nine o'clock. Anita and her husband went to bed at ten o'clock.

Dialogue: Anita is talking on the phone to Kathy.

Anita: *Hello, is Kathy home?*
Kathy: *This is Kathy.*
Anita: *Hi Kathy, this is Anita.*
Kathy: *Hi Anita. How have you been?*
Anita: *I have been fine. How was your week?*
Kathy: *Pretty busy, as usual.*
Anita: *What did you do this week?*
Kathy: *Well, I went to work everyday of course.*
Anita: *I know, what else did you do?*
Kathy: *On Monday I went swimming, on Wednesday I read a new novel.*
Anita: *That sounds like fun. I have been busy as well.*
Kathy: *What did you do last week?*
Anita: *On Monday I went shopping, on Tuesday and Wednesday I did chores.*
Kathy: *What did you do on the weekend?*
Anita: *On Saturday we went out to eat. On Sunday we went to the beach.*
Kathy: *That sounds like you had a great week.*
Anita: *Yes I did. It was nice to talk to you.*
Kathy: *Yes, it was. Thanks for calling, Anita.*
Anita: *Goodbye Kathy.*
Kathy: *Goodbye Anita. I'll call you next week.*

Questions:

1. What did Anita do on Monday?
2. Where did she go first on Monday?
3. What did she do on Tuesday
4. What did she do on Wednesday?
5. What did she do on Thursday?
6. Where did she go first on Thursday?
7. Where did she go on Friday?
8. What did she do on Saturday?
9. What did everyone have for dinner?
10. Where did they go on Sunday?

11. How was the weather?
12. What time did they all go to bed?
13. What did Kathy do on Monday?
14. What did she do on Wednesday?
15. Who called whom?
16. Who answered the phone?
17. Who will call whom next week?

Activity: Last Week

Write down what you did each day last week. Use the past tense.

Day of the week:	What did you do?
Monday	
Tuesday	
Wednesday	
Thursday	
Friday	
Saturday	
Sunday	

Now ask your classmate. Write his or her answers in the chart.

Day of the week:	What did you do?
Monday	
Tuesday	
Wednesday	
Thursday	
Friday	
Saturday	
Sunday	

Discussion Questions:

1. Who usually buys groceries for your family? What groceries does he or she buy? Where does he or she go to buy groceries?
2. Who usually does the laundry for your family? How often?
3. Do you have a garden in your house? Do you have any plants inside your house? How about any flowers?
4. Do you ever go to the post office? What do you do there?
5. Do you ever go to the bank? What do you do there?
6. Do you do yoga? What kind of exercise do you like to do? What kind of exercise do you dislike?
7. Which restaurant do you like? What do you like to order there?
8. Do you like pizza? What kind do you like? Where do you eat it?
9. Do you like to go to the beach? What do you like to do there?
10. When do you usually go to bed on Sunday nights?

Grammar Focus: Past Tense.

What did Anita do? Fill in the blanks with the past tense.

On Monday she _____ and _____ groceries. She _____ to the

supermarket and then to the outdoor market.

On Tuesday she _____ at home and _____ the laundry and _____

inside the house.

On Wednesday she _____ some gardening and _____ outside the house.

On Thursday she _____ to the post office to buy some stamps and to

send a package. Then she _____ to the bank to deposit some money.

On Friday she _____ to yoga class at the gym.

On Saturday _____ her children with their homework and then they all

_____ out to eat.

On Sunday the family _____ to the beach.

Lesson 18   Grocery Shopping

Look at these pictures. Say something about them.

On Monday Anita went grocery shopping.

On Monday Anita and her daughter Katie went to the supermarket to buy groceries for her family. There are five people in her family, so she bought a lot of groceries. People can buy many things at the supermarket. You can buy things to eat and things to drink. You can also buy many different kinds of daily goods. Daily goods are things that you and you family use everyday.

Anita always buys a lot of groceries, so she always gets a shopping cart. She bought some different kinds of meat. She bought steak, sausages, and bacon. She also bought some fish, bread, rice, cereal, and cookies. She bought a jar of pickles and she bought some canned food too. She bought three cans of tuna fish, two cans of tomato sauce, two cans of corn, and four cans of soup. She also bought some juice, milk, coffee, and tea.

She also bought some daily goods. She bought garbage bags, paper towels, toilet paper, and tissues. She bought some toothpaste, shampoo and soap as well.

After the supermarket Anita and Katie went to the outdoor market. She bought lots of fruit and vegetables for her family. She always goes to the outdoor market because the fruit and vegetables are fresher there. She bought some apples, bananas and oranges. She also bought some cabbage, carrots, broccoli, tomatoes and onions.

Dialogue: Anita is talking to her daughter Katie.

Anita: Katie, do you want to go grocery shopping with me?
Katie: Where are you going to go?
Anita: First, we will go to the supermarket and then to the outdoor market.
Katie: What do we need to buy at the supermarket?
Anita: We need to buy a lot of things. We need to make a shopping list.
Katie: I'll write the things down on the list. What do we need?
Anita: We need some meat. We need steak, sausages, and bacon. We also
    need some fish, bread, rice, cereal, and cookies.
Katie: Okay. What else do we need?
Anita: We also need a jar of pickles, three cans of tuna fish, two cans of tomato
    sauce, two cans of corn, and four cans of soup.
Katie: Okay. Do we need anything else?
Anita: We also need some juice, milk, coffee and tea.
Katie: Do we need to buy any daily goods?
Anita: Oh yes, I almost forgot. We need garbage bags, paper towels, toilet
    paper, tissues, toothpaste, shampoo, and soap.
Katie: That is a lot of stuff. We will need to get a shopping cart.
Anita: That's right. We also need to go to the outdoor market as well.
Katie: What do we need to buy there?
Anita: We need to buy some fruit and vegetables. We need some apples,
    bananas and oranges. We also need some cabbage, carrots, broccoli,
    tomatoes, and onions.
Katie: This sure is a long list. I hope we can remember everything.

Questions:

1. When did Anita go grocery shopping?
2. How many people are in her family?
3. What can you buy at the supermarket?
4. What are daily goods?
5. Why does Anita always get a shopping cart?
6. What kind of meat did she buy?
7. What else did she buy?

8. What canned food did she buy?
9. What daily goods did she buy?
10. Where did they go after the supermarket?
11. What did they buy?
12. Why does Anita always go to the outdoor market?
13. What kinds of fruit did she buy at the outdoor market?
14. What kinds of vegetables did she buy there?

Activity: Shopping List

Make a shopping list for your family. Buy everything you will need for one week. Write down how much everything will probably cost. Include things to eat, things to drink, things to cook with, and daily goods.

Item	Price

Practice with a classmate.

Ask: *What did you buy?*

Classmate answers: *I bought _____.*

Ask: *How much did it cost?*

Classmate answers: *It cost _____.*

Discussion Questions:

1. Who usually goes grocery shopping for your family? Where do they go?
2. What groceries do they usually buy?
3. How many different supermarkets can you think of? Where are they?
4. Is there an outdoor market near your house?
5. What things can you buy in an outdoor market?
6. Do you ever go to an outdoor market? What do you buy there?
7. What daily goods do you usually buy?
8. Why do people make shopping lists?
9. Do you ever make a shopping list when you go grocery shopping? Why?

10. What fresh food do you like to buy?
11. What canned foods do you like to buy?
12. Do you ever buy any frozen food? What?
13. Do you like to cook? What do you like to cook?
14. Why do people use shopping carts? Do you ever use a shopping cart?
15. What kind of toothpaste do you use?
16. What kind of soap and shampoo do you use?
17. Which groceries are more expensive? Which are cheaper?

Wine / Water   Beef / Pork   Soap / Shampoo   Fish / Shrimps
Rice / Potatoes   A can of abalone / A can of tuna   Bananas / Grapes

Grammar Focus: Match the question with the correct answer.

1. Where can I buy groceries?

   • They are in the vegetable section.

2. Which aisle are the vegetables in?

   • It is in the dairy section.

3. How much are bananas?

   • It is in the frozen food section.

4. How much is beef?

   • The total bill is $75.00

5. Where can I find milk?

   • Put them in a shopping cart.

6. Where can I buy a can of pineapples?

   • It is $3.00 per kilogram.

7. How much is the total bill?

   • At the supermarket.

8. Where can I put my groceries?

   • They are $0.75 per kilogram.

9. Where can I find ice cream?

   • They are in aisle three.

10. Where are the carrots?

    • In the canned food section.

Lesson 19   Housework

Look at these pictures. Say something about them.

Anita has a lot of housework to do.

Every week Anita does housework. She does housework on Tuesday. There are many different things to do. These things are called household chores. Anita has many chores to do every Tuesday.

First, she does the laundry. She puts the dirty clothes into the washing machine. She puts some detergent into the machine and then she turns it on. After the clothes are washed, she puts them in the clothes-dryer to dry. After they are dry, she takes the clothes out and folds them.

Next, she vacuums the living room carpet. She uses a vacuum cleaner. After Anita vacuums the carpet, she sweeps and mops the kitchen floor. Next, she sweeps the floor with a broom. Then, she gets a bucket of water and soap. She uses a mop to mop the floor with the soapy water.

Next, Anita wipes the tables. She wipes the table in the dining room. Then, she wipes the coffee table in the living room. She also wipes the counter top in the kitchen. After she wipes the tables, she wipes the windows. She uses a cloth to wipe the tables and the windows.

Next, she cleans the bathroom. She cleans the shower, the toilet, and the sink. Then, she wipes the mirror and cleans the floor. After this, Anita tidies up her bedroom. Her children clean their own rooms, so she doesn't need to.

Finally, Anita waters the plants. She likes plants and her plants all look very healthy. She knows how to take care of her plants as well as her house.

Dialogue: Anita is talking on the telephone to her friend Maria.

Maria: *Hello Anita. This is Maria.*
Anita: *Hi Maria. How are you?*
Maria: *Fine, thanks. What are you doing today?*
Anita: *Well, today is Tuesday, so it's house-cleaning day.*
Maria: *What do you have to do?*
Anita: *Well, this morning I'm going to do the laundry, then I'm going to vacuum the carpet, sweep and mop the floor, and wipe the tables and windows.*
Maria: *That is a lot of chores.*
Anita: *That's only the morning. After lunch I'm going to clean the bathroom, tidy the bedroom, and then water the plants.*
Maria: *It sounds like you're going to have a busy day.*
Anita: *Tuesdays are always busy days for me. What are you doing today?*
Maria: *Today, I am going to school. I have a report that is due on Friday.*
Anita: *It sounds like you are busy as well*
Maria: *That's right. I guess we are both busy doing different things.*
Anita: *Well, thanks for calling Maria.*
Maria: *Bye Anita. Try not to work too hard.*
Anita: *I'll try. Good-bye Maria.*

Questions:

1. When does Anita do housework?
2. What is another word for housework?
3. What does Anita do first?
4. Does she do laundry by hand?
5. How does she dry the clothes?
6. What does she do after the clothes are dry?
7. What does she do next?
8. What does she use?
9. What does she use to wipe the tables and windows?

10. What does she clean in the bathroom?
11. What does she do next?
12. Does she tidy her children's rooms? Why?
13. What does she do last?
14. How do her plants look? Why?
15. Who calls Anita?
16. Is Maria busy? What does she have to do?
17. What does she tell Anita?

Activity: Household Chores

Make a list of household chores for your family. Write down who should do which chores. Try to include chores for all your family members, including yourself. Also write down when the chores should be done.

Chore	Who should do it	When should they do it

Ask your classmate: **Who usually _____ at your house?**

Classmate answers: _____usually _____ at my house.

1. Does the laundry.
2. Vacuums the carpet.
3. Sweeps the floor.
4. Mops the floor.
5. Wipes the tables.
6. Wipes the windows.
7. Cleans the bathroom.
8. Tidies the bedrooms.
9. Waters the plants.

10._____

Discussion Questions:

1. Who does most of the chores in your house?
2. Do you do any chores? Which ones do you do?
3. Which chores do you not like to do? Why not?
4. Who takes out the garbage in your house?
5. How can you make less garbage?
6. Does your family recycle anything? What do you recycle?
7. Who does the laundry in your family? How often?
8. Do you have a clothes-dryer? How do you dry clothes?
9. Does your house have any plants? Who takes care of them?
10. Is it a good idea for all family members to do chores? Why?

11. Should housewives get paid? Why? How much should they get paid?
12. Would you like to have a housekeeper to clean your house? Why?
13. Is your bedroom tidy or messy?
14. Is your living room tidy or messy?
15. Is your house tidy or messy?
16. Do you have a vacuum cleaner in your house?
17. Does your house have carpets? Why?
18. What kind of floors do you have in your house?
19. How many bathrooms are in your house? Who usually cleans them?
20. How many bedrooms are in your house? Who tidies them?

Grammar Focus: Fill in the blanks.

What does Anita do?

1. First Anita _____ the laundry.

2. Then she _____ the carpet.

3. Then she _____ the floor.

4. Then she _____ the floor.

5. Then she _____ the tables.

6. Then she _____ the windows.

7. Then she _____ the bathroom.

8. Then she _____ the bedroom.

9. Then she _____ the plants.

Lesson 20   Gardening

On Wednesday Anita worked in the garden.

Anita enjoys gardening. Her house has a front yard and a back yard. Every Wednesday, Anita takes care of the front yard and back yard. She takes turns cutting the lawn. She cuts the front yard grass one week. Then, she cuts the back yard grass the next week. She uses a lawnmower to cut the lawn. After she has cut the grass she rakes the lawn and puts the grass into a plastic bag. Later, she will throw it away. She enjoys mowing the lawn. She likes her lawn to look nice and clean. She thinks mowing the lawn is also good exercise for her.

The front yard has a lawn and some bushes. The bushes are green. They grow next to the driveway. They also grow in front of the house. Sometimes the bushes get too big and look a little messy. When they are too big or look too messy Anita cuts them with her shears. Anita's children often leave their toys on the driveway. Anita picks up the children's toys and puts them in the garage. The garage is sometimes messy, too. So, Anita has to tidy this as well. She puts everything on a shelf or in a box in the garage.

The back yard has a lawn, some trees, and a flower garden. Every year in the spring Anita plants some new flowers in her flower garden. She thinks they look beautiful. There are some red roses, pink carnations, white lilies, and purple violets. Anita always waters them two or three times a week. On Wednesdays, she picks up any weeds that have grown in the flower garden. She really enjoys gardening and her garden looks very beautiful. She is very proud of her garden.

Dialogue: Anita is talking to her neighbor Susan.

Anita: *Hi Susan. How are you today?*
Susan: *I'm fine Anita. How are you?*
Anita: *I'm fine too.*
Susan: *I see you are working in the garden.*
Anita: *That's right. It's Wednesday today.*
Susan: *I think you always work in the garden on Wednesday.*
Anita: *That's right. There are many things to do.*
Susan: *Which lawn will you mow this week?*
Anita: *This week I will mow the front lawn.*
Susan: *Did you mow the back lawn last week?*
Anita: *Yes, I did. I mowed the back lawn last week.*
Susan: *You're flower garden looks very nice this year.*
Anita: *Thank you. I try to take good care of it.*
Susan: *What flowers do you have in it this year?*
Anita: *There are some red roses and some pink carnations.*
Susan: *They are beautiful. What are those others?*
Anita: *Those are white lilies and purple violets.*
Susan: *Everything looks great. You must be very proud of your garden.*
Anita: *I am very proud of it. It is hard work, though.*

Questions:

1. What does Anita enjoy?
2. How many yards does her house have?
3. How often does she cut the front lawn?
4. How often does she cut the back lawn?
5. What does she do after she has cut the grass?
6. Why does she enjoy mowing the lawn?
7. Where are the bushes?
8. What does Anita do when the bushes look messy?
9. What do her children sometimes do?
10. What does Anita do with their toys?

11. Why does Anita have to tidy the garage?
12. What is in the back yard?
13. What does she do every spring?
14. What kinds of flowers did she plant this year?
15. How often does she water them?
16. What does she do on Wednesdays?
17. Why is she proud of her garden?
18. Who is Susan?
19. What does Susan say about Anita's garden?

Activity: Garden Design

Look at these different gardens. What can you see? How do these gardens make you feel?

What different things can you see in these gardens? Write your ideas here.

_____

_____

_____

_____

_____

_____

On a piece of paper draw a garden. Label all the things in the garden in English. When you have finished, show your garden to your classmates.

Discussion Questions:

1.   Do you enjoy gardening? Why?
2.   Does your house have a garden? Where is it? What is in it?
3.   Do you have many plants in your house? Where are they?
4.   What flowers commonly grow in your country?
5.   What is your favorite kind of flower? What color is it?

6.   People often send flowers on special occasions.
     What flowers are appropriate for a:

     - Wedding:
     - Funeral:
     - Birthday:
     - Valentine's Day:
     - Mother's Day:
     - Romantic date:

7.   Some people enjoy gardening. Some people think gardening is too much
     trouble. What do you think?
8.   If you had a big back yard, would you rather have a swimming pool, a
     fishpond or a fountain? Why?
9.   If you had a back yard, would you let your children play baseball in it? Why?
10. If you had a flower garden, what kinds of flowers would you plant? Why?

11. What do you usually do on Wednesdays?
12. What did you do last Wednesday?
13. What will you do next Wednesday?

Grammar Focus: Fill in the blanks.

Anita _____ gardening. Her house _____ a front yard and a back yard.

Every Wednesday, Anita _____ care of the front yard and back yard. She

_____ turns cutting the lawn. She _____ the front grass one week.

Then she _____ the back yard grass the next week. She _____ a

lawnmower to _____ the lawn. After she _____ cut the grass she _____

the lawn and _____ the grass into a plastic bag. Later, she will _____it

away. She _____ mowing the lawn. She likes her lawn to look nice and

clean. She _____ mowing the lawn _____ also good exercise for her.

Lesson 21   The Post Office and the Bank

Look at these pictures. Say something about them.

On Thursday Anita went to the post office and to the bank.

The post office is usually a very busy place. There are usually many people waiting in line. They all want to do different things. Some people want to buy stamps. Some people want to send packages.

Anita needed to buy some stamps and to send a package. At the post office she talks to the clerk. The clerk was very helpful. It is her Mother's birthday soon. She bought some stamps for her mother's birthday card. She bought her mother a present and sent it in a package. She bought her Mom a cookbook. Anita hopes her Mom likes the card and present.

The bank is usually a busy place, too. People have to take a number and then wait. When your number is called you go to the teller's desk. Tellers can help you do many things. They can help you deposit money into your account. They can help you withdraw money from your account. They can help you transfer money from one account to another. They can help to handle checks. Tellers are very helpful people.

Anita needed to deposit some money into her bank account. She took a number and waited. When her number was called she went to the teller's desk. The teller helped Anita deposit money into her bank account.

Dialogue 1: Anita is at the post office. She is talking to the clerk.

Clerk: *May I help you?*
Anita: *Yes, please. I need some stamps for this card.*
Clerk: *Let me weigh it for you. That is one dollar and fifty cents.*
Anita: *Okay. Thank you.*
Clerk: *Do you need anything else?*
Anita: *Yes, please. I also need to send this package.*
Clerk: *Let me weigh it for you. That is three dollars and ten cents.*
Anita: *Here you are. That is four dollars and sixty cents.*
Clerk: *Thank you. Is that all?*
Anita: *Yes it is. Thanks for all your help.*

Dialogue 2: Anita is at the bank. She is talking to the teller.

Teller: *May I help you?*
Anita: *Yes, please. I want to deposit this money into my account.*
Teller: *Is that a savings account or a checking account?*
Anita: *I want to deposit it into my savings account.*
Teller: *Just fill out this deposit slip.*
Anita: *OK, thank you. Here you are.*
Teller: *Don't forget your account number.*
Anita: *Oh, thanks. I almost forgot.*
Teller: *Is that all? Do you need anything else?*
Anita: *No, thank you. That is all. Thanks for all your help.*

Questions:

1. Why is the post office usually a busy place?
2. What do people want to do there?
3. Where did Anita go first?
4. Why did she go there?
5. How much did the stamps for the card cost?
6. How much did it cost to send the package?
7. How much money did everything cost?
8. What was in the package?

9. What do you have to do at the bank?
10. What can bank tellers help you do?
11. What can bank tellers handle?
12. Where did Anita go after she went to the post office?
13. What did she want to do?
14. What did she have to fill out?
15. What did the teller remind her to do?
16. Did Anita need anything else at the bank?

Activity: At the Post Office

Anita bought her mother a cookbook for her birthday. She also sent her a birthday card. Think of some suitable presents for some of your friends and family members. Think about what they like or what they need. Write your ideas in the chart.

Person	Present

Activity: The Lottery

Imagine that tomorrow you will win the lottery. The jackpot is US $ Ten million. What you would like to do with all that money? How much will you spend? What will you buy? How much will you save? Fill in the chart.

Spend	Save	Other

Discussion Questions:

1. Which post office do you usually go to? Why do you go to this one?
2. What do you usually do at the post office?
3. When did you last go to the post office?
4. What did you do there?
5. Was it crowded? How long did you have to wait in line?
6. Some people like to collect stamps. Did you ever like to collect stamps?
7. What other things do you like to collect?

8. How many bank accounts do you have? Which banks do you use?
9. Which bank do you usually go to? Why do you go to this one?
10. What do you usually do at the bank?
11. When did you last go to the bank?
12. What did you do there?
13. Was it crowded? How long did you have to wait in line?
14. Which bank is nearest to where you live? Do you often go there?
15. Do you often use an ATM? What do you use it for?

16. Have you ever played the lottery?
17. Which lottery numbers would you choose? Why?

Grammar Focus: Fill in the blanks.

The post office ____ usually a very busy place. There _____ usually many people waiting in line. They all want to _____ different things. Some people want to _____ stamps. Some people want to _____ packages.

The bank _____ usually a busy place, too. People _____ to _____ a number and then _____. When your number is _____ you go to the teller desk. Tellers can _____ you _____ many things. They can help you _____ money into your account. They can help you _____ money from your account. They can help you _____ money from one account to another. They can help to _____checks. Tellers _____ very helpful people.

Lesson 22   Staying Healthy

Look at these pictures. Say something about them.

These people know that it is important to stay healthy. They always try to stay healthy. They do this by getting regular exercise, good nutrition, healthy habits, keeping a healthy attitude, and living in a clean environment.

Anita goes to Yoga class every Friday at the gym. She goes to yoga class with her sister. Anita knows that good nutrition is important for good health. She always tries to cook healthy food for her family.

Marcia enjoys aerobics. She goes to aerobics class on Mondays. She goes to the gym to do aerobics. Marcia knows that healthy habits are important for good health. She always tries to go to bed and wake up early. She always goes to bed and wakes up at regular times every day.

Freddy likes playing basketball and going dancing. He plays basketball twice a week. He plays in the park with some of his friends. Freddy knows that a good attitude is important for health. He always tries to be happy. He is seldom unhappy or sad. Freddy is always in a good mood. You can always see a smile on his face.

Kathy enjoys swimming. She swims once a week. She swims at a swimming pool near her office. She goes swimming with one of her co-workers. Kathy knows that a clean environment is important for good health. Her apartment is always very clean. She doesn't like dust and dirt. She always keeps her apartment clean and tidy. Kathy also knows that it is important to keep her neighborhood and her city clean. She never throws garbage on the ground. She also recycles and tries not to waste things at home.

Dialogue: Kathy and Freddy are talking.

Kathy: *Hi Freddy. How are you doing?*
Freddy: *I'm fine, Kathy. How are you?*
Kathy: *I'm good, thank you. Do you still play basketball?*
Freddy: *Yes I do. I play every week with some of my friends.*
Kathy: *That's great. How is work these days?*
Freddy: *Work is good. I always try to stay in a good mood.*
Kathy: *That's really important for a teacher.*
Freddy: *It's not always easy, though.*
Kathy: *Yes. I imagine it must be a hard job sometimes.*
Freddy: *I still like it though. How about you? Are you still swimming?*
Kathy: *Yes, I am. I swim once a week.*
Freddy: *Where do you swim?*
Kathy: *I swim at a pool near my office.*
Freddy: *That's great. And is your apartment still spotless?*
Kathy: *It sure is. I don't like to live in a dirty place. You know that.*
Freddy: *Maybe you can come and clean my place sometime.*
Kathy: *I don't think so Freddy. That's your responsibility.*
Freddy: *I guess you are right. Maybe I'll tidy around the house this weekend.*

Questions.

1. What do these people know?
2. How can you stay healthy?
3. What does Anita do every Friday?
4. Who does she go with?
5. What kind of food does Anita try to cook for her family?
6. What does Marcia enjoy?
7. When does she go to aerobics class?
8. What does Marcia know?
9. What does she always try to do?

10. What does Freddy like?
11. How often does he play basketball?
12. Where does he play?
13. What kind of mood is Freddy always in?
14. What can you always see on Freddy's face?

15. What does Kathy enjoy?
16. How often does she go swimming?
17. What does Kathy know?
18. Is her apartment clean or dirty?
19. What doesn't she like?
20. What does she never throw on the ground?
21. What other things does she do at home?

Activity: Healthy and Unhealthy Lifestyles

How can you have a healthy lifestyle? Write some words in the chart.

Exercise	Nutrition	Habits	Attitude	Environment

How can you have an unhealthy lifestyle? Write some words in the chart.

Exercise	Nutrition	Habits	Attitude	Environment

Look at all the information in these charts.
Is your lifestyle healthy or unhealthy?

Discussion Questions.

1. What healthy things do you eat? Why do you eat them?
2. What healthy things do you drink? Why do you drink them?
3. What unhealthy things do you eat? Why do you eat them?
4. What unhealthy things do you drink? Why do you drink them?
5. What kinds of exercise do you like to do? How often do you do them?
6. What kinds of exercise do you dislike? Why do you dislike them?
7. What time do you usually go to bed?
8. What time do you usually get up?
9. What kinds of things can people recycle? Do you ever recycle? What?
10. Are you a wasteful person? What do you waste?

11. How is your attitude? Are you usually a happy or an unhappy person?
12. What things make you happy?
13. What things make you unhappy?
14. How is your mood today? Are you in a good mood or a bad mood? Why?

Complete this sentence about your mood today.

Today I am in a _____ **mood because** _____.

Grammar Focus: Correct the mistakes in each sentence.

1. Anita go to Yoga class every Fridays out the gym.

2. Anita know that good nutrition is important for good healthy.

3. Marcia go to aerobics class in Mondays.

4. Marcia always try to go bed and wakes up early.

5. Freddy play in the park with some of his friend.

6. Freddy always try to be happily.

7. Kathy swim at a swimming pool near his office.

8. Kathy know that is important to keep her neighborhood and his city cleans.

9. She never litter or throw garbage in the ground.

10. She also recycle and try not waste things in home.

Lesson 23   Going to a Restaurant

Anita's family likes to eat Italian food.

On Saturday Anita and her family all went out to eat. They went to an Italian restaurant. The Italian restaurant is called Luigi's. It's on Park Avenue. They serve Italian food at Luigi's. The food is always delicious, so Anita and her family go there once or twice a month. On Saturday the restaurant is usually crowded, so Anita called them to make a reservation. She booked a table for four people. Her husband Frank drove to the restaurant. He parked the car in the restaurant's parking lot. This is only for customers of the restaurant.

Inside the restaurant the hostess took them to their table. They all looked at the menu to decide what they want to eat. Then, the waiter came to their table and took their order. On Saturday everyone had vegetable soup for a starter. Anita had spaghetti and meatballs, her husband had lasagna, and the children had pizza for their main course. They all had a salad for a side dish. Everyone had cola to drink. And after they were finished they all had ice cream for dessert. Anita and her husband had vanilla ice cream. The children both had chocolate.

The food was delicious as usual, and everyone was full when they finished. After Anita's husband paid the bill he left a tip on the table for the waiter. Usually the tip is fifteen or twenty percent of the price of the meal. Their meal was fifty dollars, so Anita's husband left a ten-dollar tip for the waiter.

Dialogue: The waiter is taking the family's order.

Waiter: *Are you ready to order?*
Frank: *Yes we are. I'll have lasagna please.*
Waiter: *And for you, madam?*
Anita: *I'll have spaghetti please.*
Waiter: *And for the children.*
Children: *We want pizza!*
Waiter: *OK, what kind of pizza would you like?*
Children: *We want pepperoni pizza, please.*
Waiter: *Fine. And would you like a starter?*
Anita: *We all would like vegetable soup, please.*
Waiter: *Fine. And would you like salad, too?*
Frank: *Yes please. With Thousand Island dressing.*
Waiter: *OK. So you all want vegetable soup and salad with Thousand Island dressing. One lasagna, one spaghetti and one pepperoni pizza. Would you like something to drink?*
Anita: *I think we all would like cola, please.*
Waiter: *Okay, I'll bring your soups first*
Frank: *Thank you very much. We are all very hungry!*

Questions:

1. Where did Anita's family go on Saturday?
2. Where is Luigi's?
3. Do they serve Chinese food at Luigi's?
4. How often do they go to Luigi's?
5. Why do they like to go there?
6. Why did Anita make a reservation?
7. Where did they park?

8. Who took their order?
9. What did they have for a starter?
10. What did Anita have for her main course?
11. What did Anita's husband have for his main course?
12. What did the children have for their main course?
13. What did they all have to drink?
14. What did they have for a side dish?
15. What did they have for dessert?
16. What kind of ice cream did they have?

17. How much was the bill?
18. How much tip did Anita's husband leave?

Activity: Matching International Foods

At what kind of restaurant can you find these international foods?

Food	Restaurant
Sushi and Sashimi	
Pizza and Spaghetti	
Burritos and Nachos	
Shrimp Curry and Coconut Juice	
Steak and Salad	
Kimchi and Spicy Shrimp Soup	
Gong Bao Chicken and Fried Rice	
Veggie Burger	
Steamed Cod and Clam Soup	
Frogs Legs and Snails	

Activity: Make a Menu

On a piece of paper make a menu for a restaurant.

Include starters, soup, main courses, side dishes, drinks, and desserts.

Try to think of at least three for each.

Don't forget to include the price for each item on your menu.

Now, order something from a classmate's menu.

Discussion Questions:

1. Do you usually eat breakfast at home or eat out? What do you usually have for breakfast?
2. Do you usually eat lunch at home or eat out? What do you usually have?
3. Do you usually eat dinner at home or eat out? What do you usually have?

4. What kind of restaurant do you like to go to?
5. What is the name? Where is it?
6. What kind of food do they serve?
7. What do you usually order?
8. Who do you usually go with?
9. When did you last go there?
10. What did you have? How was it?
11. Why do you usually go there?
12. Do you ever leave the waiter or waitress a tip? Why?

13. What restaurants do you know that serve international or Western food?
14. Do you ever go there? What international food do you like to eat?

15. Would you rather have Sushi and Sashimi or Frogs Legs and Snails? Why?
16. Would you prefer a Burrito and Nachos or Shrimp Curry and Coconut Juice?
17. Would you rather have Steak and Salad or Kimchi and Spicy Shrimp Soup?
18. Would you prefer Gong Bao Chicken and Fried Rice or Veggie Burger?
19. Would you prefer Steamed Cod and Clam Soup or Pizza and Spaghetti?

Grammar Focus: Fill in the blank with a past tense verb.

On Saturday Anita _____ her children with their homework and then they all

_____ out to eat. They _____ to an Italian restaurant.

Anita _____ the restaurant to make a reservation. She _____ a

table for four people. The food _____ delicious as usual. After Anita's husband

_____ the bill he _____ the waitress a tip on the table. Their meal

_____ fifty dollars, so Anita's husband _____ ten dollars for the waitress.

Lesson 24   Going to the Beach

Look at these pictures. Say something about them.

Anita and her family like to go to the beach.

On Sunday Anita and her family went to the beach. They drove their car to the beach. It took about an hour to get there. When they got there the beach was crowded. There were many people there. So, Anita and her family had to look for a nice place to sit on the sand. When they found a nice spot they put down a blanket and sat down. The weather was good on Sunday. It was sunny and warm. They all wore hats to protect their faces from the sun. They all wore swimming suits and T-shirts. Everyone remembered to put on sunscreen to prevent sunburn.

At the beach Anita read a book. Her husband and the children played in the water. Anita had prepared a picnic for them to eat at the beach. When everyone was hungry, they opened the cooler and ate lunch. They ate sandwiches, salad, potato chips, and fruit. After lunch they were very full and a little sleepy so they took a nap. In the afternoon they took a walk on the beach. They saw many people there. Some people were swimming. Some were sunbathing. Some were flying kites. Some were playing volleyball. Some were playing Frisbee. The beach is always a very lively place.

They all had a good time at the beach. But when they got home that evening they were all very tired, so they all went to bed early. The children went to bed at nine o'clock. Anita and her husband went to bed at ten o'clock.

Dialogue: Anita and her husband are talking at the beach.

Anita: *This looks like a good place.*
George: *Yes. Let's put down the blanket and the cooler here.*
Anita: *It's very hot today and the sun is very bright.*
George: *We should all put some sunscreen on.*
Anita: *That's right. We don't want to get sunburn.*
George: *I think I'll go in the water with the kids. Do you want to come too?*
Anita: *No thanks. I'm going to sit here and read my book.*
George: *Okay. We should have lunch in a little while.*
Anita: *I brought a picnic. I brought sandwiches, salad, potato chips, and fruit.*
George: *That sounds great.*
Anita: *Be careful in the water.*
George: *Don't worry. The kids and I are good swimmers.*
Anita: *I know you can all swim very well. But sometimes the waves are big.*
George: *You're right. We will all be very careful in the water.*
Anita: *All right. Have a good time.*
George: *We will. Enjoy your book.*

Questions:

1. What did Anita do on Sunday?
2. How did they get there?
3. How long did it take?
4. Were there many people at the beach?
5. How was the weather on Sunday?
6. What did they wear at the beach?
7. Why did they put on sunscreen?
8. What did they do before lunch?
9. What did Anita warn them about?

10. What did they have for lunch?
11. How did they feel after lunch?
12. What did they do in the afternoon?
13. What were the other people doing?
14. How did they feel when they got home?
15. What time did the children go to bed?
16. What time did Anita and her husband go to bed?

Beach Rules.
No camping.
No fires.
No Frisbee.
No volleyball.
No alcohol.
No dogs.
No swimming after dark.

Look at this sign of beach rules.
Do you think these regulations are reasonable? Why?
What other rules should be on the sign? Why?

Activity: Going To the Beach

You and your family are going to the beach. Make a list of 10 things you will take. Write down why you need to take each thing.

Item to take	Why do you need it

Plan an activity schedule for a day at the beach. Write down what you will do. Begin in the morning and finish in the evening. Write eight things.

1.

2.

3.

4.

5.

6.

7.

8.

Discussion Questions:

1. Where is the nearest beach to your house? Do you ever go there? Why?
2. Where is there a nice beach? Do you ever go there? Why?
3. What do people like to do at the beach? See if you can make a list of at least ten things. Which of these do you like to do?
4. Why are some beaches dirty?
5. What kind of litter and garbage can you see at the beach?
6. How can people help to keep the beach clean?
7. Do you think it's important to keep the beach clean? Why?

8. Can you swim? Where did you learn? Where do people learn to swim?
9. Do you prefer to swim in a swimming pool or in the ocean? Why?
10. What are some other places people can go swimming in?
11. What kinds of animals live in the ocean?
12. What other things can you see in the ocean?
13. Do you like seafood? What kinds do you prefer? How often do you eat seafood? Which places have good seafood?
14. Where do you usually eat seafood? Do you know any famous or popular seafood restaurants?

Grammar Focus: Fill in the blanks with the past tense verb.

At the beach Anita _____ a book. Her husband and the children _____ in the

water. Anita _____a picnic for them to eat at the beach. When

everyone _____ hungry, they _____the cooler and _____ lunch. They

_____sandwiches, salad, potato chips and fruit. After lunch they _____ very full

and a little sleepy so they _____ a nap. In the afternoon they _____ a walk on the

beach. They _____many people there. Some people _____swimming. Some

_____sunbathing. Some _____ flying kites. Some _____ playing volleyball. Some

_____ playing Frisbee. The beach is very lively on Sundays. They all _____a

good day at the beach. But, when they _____ home that evening they _____ all

tired, so they all _____ to bed early. The children _____ to bed at nine o'clock.

Anita and her husband _____ at bed at ten o'clock.

Made in the USA
Middletown, DE
02 January 2015